THE
KARASIK
SEMINAR
SYSTEM

SEMINAR
SUCCESS
MANUAL

CONTENTS

PART ONE: GETTING STARTED WITH THE KARASIK SEMINAR SYSTEM

*Once you familiarize yourself with this manual,
learn about the various approaches to seminars,
and find out how to create successful seminars, you will be
ready to focus on the types of seminars you
think will work best for you.*

CHAPTER 1.
OVERVIEW OF THE KARASIK
SEMINAR SYSTEM

The Karasik Seminar System has only one purpose: to dramatically and quickly increase your net income. You will create an emotional bond with your participants because you will explore the issues, people, and activities that are important to them. Because you focus on what is important to them, you will establish rapport and trust easily. New business opportunities will arise effortlessly.

The Karasik Seminar System is a complete turn-key system designed to enable you to increase your business with one of the most effective and proven strategies: seminar marketing.

Three steps will help you get started.

First, read this Seminar Success Manual. The purpose of the manual is to provide you with the precise skills and education you need to get in front of qualified prospects.

The manual focuses on three venues: client events, public events, and in-house events. Each venue will produce lucrative new business for you. Each seminar venue requires unique marketing pieces, scripts, time lines, and logistical tactics. You will find all of them in this manual.

Each seminar approach will be examined in detail. A time line will guide you through each step of the seminar marketing process and will help you to replicate your success.

Part Six of the manual, Marketing Resources, contains the phone scripts and marketing documents you will need to maximize your results. You will also be provided with information about the best companies, contacts, and vendors to help you execute the seminar marketing process.

For greatest effectiveness, share this manual with each person involved in marketing your seminar. Strive to delegate as many marketing activities as possible.

Second, review all the other elements included in the Karasik Seminar System, which are as follows:

a. Leader's Guide for the seminar *Taking Control of Your Financial Future*
The Leader's Guide gives you the script associated with each slide, guidelines for facilitating each activity, and tips for maximizing your success. The guide also includes strategies and techniques for delivering a dynamic seminar.

b. PowerPoint® Presentation CD
This presentation consists of high-impact, full-color graphics that will reinforce your message and your professionalism. You can customize and amend the presentation with slides or information (compliance approved) relevant to your business model, product focus, or presentation style.

c. Marketing Campaign CD
The marketing CD-ROM contains all of the resources in Part Six of this manual so that you can have easy access to them and customize them. The CD includes marketing letters, advertisements, direct mail promotion pieces, confirmation letters, evaluations forms, and lots more.

Third, implement a plan. Decide which types of seminars you will conduct, and follow the detailed plans provided. Of course you will customize all of the scripts and marketing documents to fit you. By refining and perfecting the process each time you conduct a seminar, you will continue to increase your profitability.

Throughout this manual you will find three symbols:

means that you are about to be given a valuable contact that you can use to help maximize your success.

means that you are being provided with a great idea or tip.

means that you are being given a marketing resource, such as a letter or phone script.

CHAPTER 2.
CHOOSING THE MOST
PROFITABLE SEMINAR VENUE

Most financial professionals have a limited view of seminar opportunities. You will learn about the three lucrative seminar venues. Each one has its advantages and disadvantages.

The Client-Event Seminar
The Client-Event Seminar is marketed to your existing clients as well as to the people they invite.

Advantages. The most outstanding advantage of the client event strategy is that it generates referrals. It provides a painless way of getting to meet more prospects through referrals. Just as important, the quality of the referrals equals the quality of your invited clients.

In other words, if you invite only your ideal clients, the ones you would like to clone, and you ask them to invite people like themselves, you will have the opportunity to expand your universe of highly profitable clients and grow your business exponentially.

It's important to look at this a little deeper. If you currently have one hundred clients and would like to double your income, you don't need one hundred more clients. What you actually need are twenty-five clients just like your top twenty. Obviously, obtaining referrals is one of the most effective methods of increasing your business. The client seminar offers an efficient system for meeting lots of referrals quickly.

The second advantage of the client-event seminar is that you will expand your relationship with existing clients. The client-event seminar can help you to build trust and create opportunities to cross sell other products and services. It is not unusual for clients to attend a client event and say before they leave, "Oh, by the way, I need to talk to you about something that just came up. When can we get together?"

The third advantage is that you will be adding value to your relationships. When your clients examine and explore their deeper values and life goals and share them with you, your relationship with them will deepen. Client retention will be a given, and you will be more likely to get unsolicited referrals.

The fourth advantage of client-event seminars is its ease, efficiency, and low cost of promotion. You can fill the room with just five or ten phone calls. The only other expenses are the room and a few refreshments.

You do not need to serve a meal; in fact doing so is actually an obstacle because of the logistics. Your program will run too long if you serve dinner and then conduct an hour and a half seminar. And the workbooks can present a problem when food is served.

If your office has a conference room, you can use it to save money on a room rental and further reduce the costs of the client seminar. If you do rent a room, you will only need a small one that holds about twenty people.

The final advantage of the client-event seminar is it gives you a chance to create strategic alliances with CPAs.

> Ask your clients to invite their CPAs to the event. It's the perfect way for you to initiate such relationships. After the event, you can call the CPAs, meet, and discuss ways you can work together to help the client you share and ways you can help each other professionally.

Disadvantages. The primary drawback of this seminar approach is the possibility that the audience you can attract might be limited. This would be the case if you were in the early stage of your career and had only a few clients or if you had only a few clients you considered good enough to want to clone. The strategic alliance tactic is one answer to this problem, but it is also limited if you have very few clients.

The second problem is how comfortable you are with your clients. If you have given your clients little attention or you feel they are not thoroughly satisfied with your services, you might be hesitant to invite them in as a group.

The best solution to this problem is to begin immediately to service, communicate, and build relationships with your best clients. Certainly all new clients can be offered this seminar as a dynamic way to get started.

The In-House Seminar

The participants of an in-house seminar have been assembled by an organization or group, usually with little or no input or effort from you. The seven most readily accessible inhouse settings include:

1. Trade and professional association meetings. Many of these associations welcome speakers who can provide financial information and insight to their members.

2. Adult and continuing education programs. Practically every university, community college, high school district, and community recreation department offers some form of noncredit adult education courses, including financial education courses. In many large cities, privately owned seminar companies offer adult education not affiliated with any institution. The companies distribute free catalogs throughout the city, offering a wide array of personal and professional development courses. Among these are seminars on financial education.

3. Service Clubs and Fraternal Organizations. Many local groups, such as Rotary, Kiwanis, Lions, and Elks, bring in speakers and provide an excellent opportunity for presenting your program.

4. Church and religious groups. In an effort to serve the far-ranging needs of their congregations, almost every religious organization in the United States offers nonreligious education programs.

5. Corporate programs. Many corporations have gradually reduced their direct involvement in the financial security of their employees. Education is a simple and cost-effective contribution they can offer. Therefore, many corporations promote financial education programs during lunch breaks and after work.

6. Nonprofit organizations. These groups meet regularly and may offer the

perfect venue in which to speak and create win-win opportunities, such as planned giving programs. Nonprofit memberships include many affluent people who have a commitment to community service.

7. Senior centers and senior living facilities. Senior centers always seek programs relevant to the lives of their members. Financial seminars are popular with these groups.

Advantages. There are two significant advantages to staging in-house seminars. First, you employ the foremost marketing priority: targeting. In most cases, the in-house market is targeted by definition.

For example, if physicians are your target market, it would be ideal to speak at a local professional meeting of physicians. Similarly if your target market is older people, a senior center would present the most targeted group available. If your ideal client profile includes certain values or lifestyle qualities, church groups could be the most targeted setting for you.

The second advantage is promotion costs. Marketing costs associated with inhouse programs are practically nonexistent. Because the meeting or gathering has been arranged by the organization or group, you will not need to invest in promoting the event.

The only investment will be a few dollars to mail a media kit to the decision maker. The low-cost or no-cost promotion aspect of in-house seminars is particularly important to the new advisor who has limited resources for prospecting. Basically all you have to do is show up.

Disadvantages. In-house seminars suffer from two drawbacks. The first is the ability to duplicate the system. Let's assume real estate professionals are your target market. After you speak at all the real estate meetings in your area, you will probably need to let some time pass before you approach them again. This is also probably true for groups such as chambers of commerce.

This disadvantage does not hold true for organizations that attract a flow of ever changing participants. For example, adult education groups continually attract new participants to their programs. In fact these programs become ongoing marketing opportunities once you have proven yourself. They will market your program one or two times every year.

The other disadvantage is lack of control. Everything, from knowing the names of the participants to logistics and time allotment, will be out of your control. Some venues, such as corporate programs, make direct solicitation for appointments difficult or impossible. When speaking to an assembled group, creative closing strategies need to be employed.

Most of these negative aspects can be minimized or overcome, but they need to be addressed in order to make in-house programs a profitable marketing strategy.

The Public Seminar

The public seminar is the most common venue. In fact, many advisors view this as the only venue for presenting seminars.

Public seminars are events promoted through direct mail, print advertisements, or telephone solicitation. These programs are usually conducted at hotels, restaurants, libraries, and other public places.

Advantages. The public seminar provides you with a system you can duplicate. You can control all aspects of seminar promotion, content, and delivery. The public seminar casts a wide net for new prospects. A percentage of those attending the program are likely to be qualified prospects. The public seminar is attractive to new advisors who may focus more on quantity and less on quality.

Disadvantages. Because the public seminar attracts a wide variety of participants, many attendees will not be high-quality prospects and will not fit your ideal client profile.

Although many list brokers promise lists of high-net-worth clients, every list in fact includes a range of prospects. Obviously, print advertisements attract an equally wide range of prospects. More experienced advisors must set qualifying standards to avoid this problem.

The other significant disadvantage of public seminars is the cost. Promotion will more than likely be in the thousands of dollars. This is not a problem if your events are profitable, but two or three unsuccessful events can become very costly and will be a strong deterrent to pursuing this venue.

Choosing the Best Venue for You

Each of these seminar formats offers opportunities and has limitations. You need to choose the venue or venues that best fit your business model, your experience, and your geographic location. But ultimately, your hunger to grow your business will determine your marketing plan.

The client-event seminar is appropriate for practically all financial professionals. Because the client-event seminar is targeted, referral based, relatively inexpensive, and easy to implement, it is an ideal format. If you are a more experienced financial advisor who has been in business for years, you might have enough ideal clients to roll out a oneyear marketing plan consisting of client-event seminars alone. The new clients you generate will become participants in your next round of client-event seminars.

If you are new to the business or do not have enough ideal clients, public seminars offer you the opportunity to throw out the net. Depending on your business model, you will need to set qualifying standards. Because public seminars are costly to promote, you will need to continually monitor the return on investment, the ROI. The ROI needs to be the determining issue in making your venue decision. Profitability, not cost, should guide your decision.

Most financial advisors should continually pursue a variety of in-house seminar opportunities in addition to client-event seminars. Depending on your target market and your geographic region, some in-house seminars might be one-shot opportunities while others might be ongoing possibilities. For example, only one or two local professional association meetings might be appropriate for you to speak at, but you might be able to offer an ongoing program at a local corporation.

CHAPTER 3.
THE SEVEN IMMUTABLE LAWS
OF SEMINAR SUCCESS

Seminars can be one of the most effective strategies for gathering assets. Sadly, many financial advisors abandon their seminar marketing efforts when results fail to live up to expectations. The secret to success is to obey a few immutable laws for achieving seminar success.

The Law of Relationships

Too many financial professionals focus on the incorrect intention. It's not about education, it's not about public speaking, it's not about fancy slide presentations, and it's not about displaying how much you know. Seminar selling is about one thing only: initiating and nurturing relationships.

All decisions relevant to your seminar efforts should be based on the Law of Relationships. Repeatedly ask yourself: How will this affect my ability to build relationships? Will it have a positive or negative effect? This includes every element, from your marketing material to choosing a seminar room to setting up the chairs to your preseminar activities to seminar materials to presentation format and so forth.

A variety of ideal opportunities exists to establish and build relationships. Call prospects during registration. Confirm the appointment, too. During the half hour before and after the seminar, make contact with your guests in an informal, personal way. Do not squander the time by talking to an assistant or a guest speaker. Obey the Law of Relationships and closing will occur naturally, as part of a process, rather than as an isolated event.

The Law of Emotion

People buy for emotional reasons and justify their purchases with logic. This applies to all buying decisions, including buying your services. Keep this in mind when delivering your seminar. If you fail to engage the emotions of the audience, you risk losing their attention and you risk losing appointments.

Your seminar might be filled with important concepts and extremely relevant data, but you will not make the sale if you fail to connect with prospects emotionally. The sales adage "People don't care about how much you know until they know how much you care" applies to seminar selling as much as to any other kind of selling. Connect with their hearts, and their minds will follow.

The Law of Trust

Trust is the most important emotion to generate throughout the seminar selling process. The only real objection in any selling situation is "I don't trust you." Keep your attention on the needs and concerns of your participants, and you will establish trust easily and effortlessly. Focus on what's important to your audience, and strive to remain people centered rather than product centered. Your products and services will sell themselves when trust is established.

The Law of Involvement

The most powerful seminars feel more like a conversation than a speech. Make an effort to create a feeling of rapport with your audience. Seminar content, activities, materials, slides, room logistics, and so forth should all be created or adjusted to optimize affinity with your audience.

The Law of Competency

Seminar success is not about luck. It's about competency. Competency is not an accident; it is the result of study and skill development. It is essential that you become a student of the four major elements of seminar selling: presentation design, seminar marketing, seminar delivery, and follow-up. Competency leads to confidence.

You will excel in some seminar selling skills, and you will need to give others more attention. Remain open to grow and continually refine your skills, and you will be rewarded with increasingly higher levels of success.

The Law of Target Marketing

Who are your ideal seminar participants, and how will you create opportunities to present your program to them? This manual will focus on the three seminar venues and how to target market in each of them. You will be provided with proven strategies and techniques for target marketing in each venue.

Always keep in mind that there is no one right marketing answer. You need to choose, apply, and customize your seminar marketing strategies and techniques based on your target market as well as your location, experience, business model, products, services, and so forth.

The Law of ROI

Obviously, the most important measure of your seminar success is your return on investment. How much money did your seminar generate in relation to your investment? Evaluate based on profitability. One new client who results in $50,000 in revenue is more valuable than five clients worth five thousand each. Avoid getting distracted by less important numbers such as how many seats were filled or how much money you spent on your direct mail campaign.

Use these seven laws as guideposts for making decisions. Share these concepts with everyone who helps you in your seminar efforts. Obey the seven immutable laws of seminar success, and you will increase your results substantially.

CHAPTER 4.
THREE CRITICAL SUCCESS STRATEGIES

Regardless of your seminar venue, size, or target audience, you need to implement three strategies to insure ongoing success.

Success Strategy One

Systematize and document. It is almost impossible to fail with seminar selling. Very few seminars do not result in profits. And yet most advisors drop seminars from their marketing plans. Why? Because they get bogged down in the process and get overwhelmed by the details and implementation.

You can avoid this obstacle to ongoing success if you systematize and document each and every part of the process. Each element in the process – who to call, what to say, what to send, when to send, and so forth – needs to be assembled in a procedures manual. Begin writing down each step with the intention of delegating it or outsourcing it.

You are well on your way to creating your procedures manual with the information in this manual. Take the relevant scripts, letters, checklists, and so forth, and customize them for your own application. By customizing, systematizing, and documenting, you will create your own seminar machine.

You also need to document your results. Keep precise records regarding seminar costs, dates, locations, appointments, and new business opportunities. These records will give you the information you need to refine your process, improve efficiency, and increase profitability.

Success Strategy Two

Employ contact management. Seminar selling will create a steady stream of new prospects who will need to be contacted. Each prospect has an associated and quantifiable marketing cost. If you drop the ball on contacting them during the marketing process, you will seriously threaten you net income.

Computerized contact management enables you to implement and include important marketing elements quickly and easily. Various contact management systems are available. Some have been specifically designed for financial advisors, and some are more generic. When choosing a software package for contact management, be sure it offers these features:

1. The capacity to include relevant prospect data. This includes the obvious information, such as name, address, phone, and e-mail, and also includes background information. It is essential that you gather and record as much information as possible from the moment of contact. This includes personal information, such as hobbies, family, recreational interests, and favorite charities, as well as financial information such as past experience with financial advisors and investments. Imagine having records and knowing, before the seminar begins, who is a do-it- yourselfer with very low potential and who is a hot prospect. You will be able to invest your time and energy on the best prospects. You will also be able to use the data you have gathered to build rapport and create relationships. And, when prospects become clients, the information will be essential to your ability to serve them on a long-term basis.

2. Data base capabilities. The contact management software should be capable of managing your mailing list and creating mailing labels. It should allow you to create fields based on criteria. For example, you might want to pull up a list of past participants and mail them a special invitation.

3. Activity management. Contact management systems have alarms that signal when a follow-up is necessary. This can be flagged as a phone call, letter, email, or any activity that is a next step for converting a prospect into a client.

Contact management software enables you to implement every step of the marketing process in a timely manner. It minimizes the chance of forgetting or losing track of what needs to be done next.

 One of the most efficient and easy-to-use contact management software programs is Salesforce, which you can find at the Web site www.salesforce.com.

Success Strategy Three

Stay in it for the long run. To do this, you must set up a seminar marketing plan rather than promoting one event at a time. Your results will snowball. You need a long-term seminar schedule for several reasons. There will always be lots of people with busy schedules who want to attend. If you keep conducting seminars, they will probably show up eventually. By the way, many of the busy people have great potential and make ideal prospects for you. When you maintain a continuous seminar schedule, you give prospects more than one chance to see you. Many people take a lot of time to make decisions. Past participants should always be invited to your future events. All studies of selling have shown that you often have to ask for the order a few times.

And finally, your ongoing seminars become a marketing technique to get lucrative in-house opportunities. Your seminars showcase you. Invite representatives from corporations, adult education programs, church groups, and other organizations to attend. Your live presentation will land an opportunity that could have taken months to obtain if you were marketing with just the telephone and direct mail.

PART TWO: THE CLIENT EVENT PLANNING GUIDE

Part Two provides you with the strategies and techniques you need to conduct successful client events.

CHAPTER 5.
THE CLIENT-EVENT SEMINAR TIMETABLE

Your client-event seminar requires a comprehensive success plan that you should implement in a timely fashion. Use the following timetable and checklist to guide you through the process, beginning ten to twelve weeks prior to the event.

Some steps in your comprehensive plan will require much less time the second or third time around. And by the time you prepare for your third seminar, you may be able to completely eliminate some steps, such as rehearsing. Also, as mentioned previously, tasks should be delegated whenever possible, allowing you to focus on your primary role as a relationship builder.

Note that the time line is not written in stone. You need to adapt and customize each and every step to fit your business model, clientele, geographic area, and so forth. The times given provide a safe framework that allows for problems, mistakes, and unexpected events that can have a negative impact on your program. Begin with the time line below, and then create your own based on your ability to execute each of the steps.

10 to 12 Weeks before the Event
[ ] Step 1. Create your invitation list.
[ ] Step 2. Assemble your team.
[ ] Step 3. Select and book the event location.

8 to 10 Weeks before the Event

[ ] Step 4. Prepare your seminar materials.

[ ] Step 5. Prepare your presentation.

[ ] Step 6. Plan your audiovisual needs.

[ ] Step 7. Invite your clients and request referrals.

4 Weeks before the Event

[ ] Step 8. Follow up with referrals by phone, email and mail.

2 Weeks before the Event

[ ] Step 9. Confirm client and referral attendance by phone and email.

1 Week before the Event

[ ] Step 10. Review and rehearse your presentation.

[ ] Step 11. Confirm all event details.

Day before the Event

[ ] Step 12. Confirm attendance of participants by phone.

CHAPTER 6.
HOW TO CONDUCT A
SUCCESSFUL CLIENT-EVENT
SEMINAR

The preparation for a client event consists of twelve steps. Each one must be understood and implemented properly to maximize your results.

Step 1. Create your invitation list.
Base your invitation list on the following five criteria:

    a. Clients you would like to clone. The client event, properly implemented, will generate referrals. People tend to know people like themselves; therefore you should invite your ideal clients because they are more likely to generate ideal referrals.

    b. Clients who are "believers." You want to invite clients who are generally supporters of your approach and are satisfied with you and your services. They believe in what you do and how you do it. These clients are likely to provide invaluable third party endorsements that can quickly transform prospects into clients.

    c. Clients you seek to expand your relationship with. These are clients you currently do business with on a limited scale only but to whom you would like to cross sell additional products or services. For example, you might have sold a client an insurance product and would like to offer an investment product or vice versa.

    d. Clients you would like to show your appreciation to. The client event is the perfect vehicle for saying thank you. It is one of the most powerful techniques for creating an emotional bond with your clients, a bond that will position you to request referrals or, even better, receive unsolicited referrals at a later date.

e. Strategic partners. The client event provides the perfect environment in which to meet partners who can help you leverage your marketing efforts. Use this event to initiate these relationships by asking your clients to invite their accountants and attorneys. The client event is a unique opportunity to be viewed in the most favorable light.

Step 2. Assemble your team.

Decide who will be involved in your seminar selling efforts. Seminar selling consists of two components: the front end and the back end.

Ideally, you will be the person up front. When you present the seminar yourself, you position yourself to create relationships, which is your goal. If you choose to use guest presenters or share the responsibility with others, be sure they understand their role. They need to defer to you and refer to you as the ultimate authority.

It is always best to enlist assistance and delegate any tasks not directly involved in creating or building relationships – the back end tasks. One of the major impediments to ongoing seminar success is the time and energy required to execute successful events.

Small client seminars are relatively easy to implement, but if your events are larger or if you are producing lots of them, you need to consider developing your staff; if you don't have a staff available, then consider hiring support personnel specifically for your events.

Create an event procedure manual that contains the exact steps taken for each event. Include the names and numbers of locations, vendors, and other relevant contacts. This procedure manual will save you incredible amounts of time if you change personnel. Remember: you should not be involved in minimum-wage tasks.

Step 3. Select and book the event location.

Your event location reflects on you and can have a huge impact on the outcome of your seminar. Evaluate your choice of location by considering these questions:

a. Will the event site be perceived as special? A local hotel meeting room might work well for a public seminar, but generally it will not be viewed as special. On the other hand, the local country club might be seen as more out of the ordinary.

b. Is the site convenient? Consider factors such as drive time, distance, possible traffic problems, and parking.

c. Is the site private and quiet? Some locations offer a variety of function rooms. A boisterous bachelor party in the next room can have a disastrous effect on your event.

d. Are there enough food choices? If you decide to offer food at your client event, will you have enough choices to accommodate a variety of tastes? Ideally, three dishes should be available: meat or chicken, fish, and vegetarian.

> If you want to be sure your choice of a venue will be well received, ask four or five of your clients for suggestions. Even if you do not use their suggestions, they will feel you value their opinion.

e. Will the room work well for a seminar? Some rooms work well for dining but lack the logistics needed for seminars, such as proper lighting, equipment for slides or sound, or layout for unobstructed viewing.

f. What is the cost factor? The difference in price between an impressive venue and a mediocre one can be minimal when you consider the return on your investment. On the other hand, it is wise to shop around to be sure you get the best quality possible for your dollar.

Step 4. Prepare your seminar materials.

Seminar materials include everything related to the seminar. Decide which of the following materials you will distribute before or during your event, and prepare them as needed.

a. Marketing materials. Do you have your invitation, confirmation letters, phone scripts, and follow-up letters customized and prepared?

b. Workbooks. Do you have enough workbooks for your event?

c. Organizational material. Will you distribute any information about your organization?

d. Product material. Will you distribute marketing material about a specific product?

e. Evaluation forms. Will you need evaluation forms?

f. Client gifts. Would you like to offer a special little gift to express your appreciation to your clients and others attending the event?

Step 5. Prepare your presentation.

Review the following elements and take appropriate action to customize your presentation as needed.

a. Would you like to include additional slides or more technical information?

b. Might you add some personal experiences or stories to your presentation to reinforce your message? One financial adviser tells a moving story about a person in the early stages of a debilitating physical problem, who needs to adjust some financial matters. The conclusion of the story reveals the person as his mother.

c. Have you adapted the presentation to your audience? For example, if your group consists of retirees as opposed to people who are preparing to retire, you might need to customize your presentation accordingly.

Step 6. Plan your audiovisual needs.

Slide projectors can be rented or purchased. In either case, explore your options and make the necessary arrangements for your event date. Some locations, such as hotels, have audiovisual equipment on hand; be sure to request it in advance.

Step 7. Invite your clients, and request referrals.

The client-event seminar requires the shortest lead time of the three venues. It is best to market your seminar about six weeks before the event.

If you conduct relatively small events with only select clients who fit the criteria in step one, you can use the telephone to fill the seats.

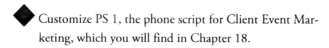 Customize PS 1, the phone script for Client Event Marketing, which you will find in Chapter 18.

If, on the other hand, you will conduct larger events with less emphasis on cloneworthy clients, you can consider using direct mail as your marketing technique.

◆ Customize MD 1, the Client Invitation Letter, which you will find in Chapter 19.

Every client event represents the perfect opportunity to generate high-quality referrals. Ideally, half of the participants should be referrals.

◆ Customize PS 2, PS 3, or PS 4, the phone scripts for Referral Generation, found in Chapter 18.

If your clients find it difficult to come up with people they can invite to your event, use the phone script for helping clients identify referrals.

◆ See PS 6, the phone script for Handling Referral Objections, in Chapter 18.

If your client does not want to make a phone call to invite the referral to the seminar, customize the letter in MD 3, and mail it to the people your client believes would profit from the seminar.

◆ See MD 3, the Referral Invitation Letter, found in Chapter 19.

Step 8. Follow up with referrals by phone and mail.

After requesting referrals from your clients, follow up by calling your clients again to collect the names of the people they have invited. You will need the names, addresses, and phone numbers of the referred guests so that you can confirm their reservations.

If your client is stuck and can't seem to come up with anyone to invite, go back to PS 6, the phone script for Handling Referral Objections.

Step 9. Confirm clients and referrals by phone and mail.

You will need the final list for planning the meal or refreshments, setting up the event room, preparing seminar materials, and so forth. Phone all the event participants to confirm that they will attend. This is also a good time to confirm food choices, if you are serving a meal.

 See PS 10, the phone script for Final Confirmation, in Chapter 18.

Step 10. Review and rehearse your presentation.

It's much easier to feel relaxed when you have taken the time to prepare properly. Review your slides, script, and seminar activities. Rehearse your presentation until you feel comfortable giving it. Accept the fact that you will improve with time.

Step 11. Confirm all event details.

This includes but is not limited to the following:

    a. Location and food. Provide the facility with the final participant count, event agenda, refreshment needs, meal choices, room setup, and other needs.

    b. Audiovisual. If you will rent equipment, confirm the delivery time and setup. Make sure you have your presentation and a backup.

    c. Program materials. Prepare and pack up all program workbooks and materials. d. Speaker. If other speakers will participate in your presentation, confirm all the details with them.

Step 12. Confirm participants by phone.

As a further precaution to prevent or limit no-shows, every client and referral should be called and confirmed.

 See chapter 13 in *How to Market to High-Net-Worth Households* by Paul Karasik for a detailed description of the ETM – Event Team Meeting – and how to conduct it. This book also contains a wealth of information on harnessing the power of the clientevent seminar to create a flow of ideal referrals. It is available online at www.paulkarasik.com.

CHAPTER 7.
THE CLIENT APPRECIATION EVENT

The client appreciation event is one of the most effective strategies for creating client loyalty and a steady stream of referrals. When it comes to client appreciation events, there is no limit on creativity.

The following guidelines will help you to conduct successful client appreciation events:

1. Avoid letting your event get lost during the holiday season, when it will seem more like a holiday party than an appreciation event.
2. Consider making it a yearly special event. You can pick a general date, like the first weekend in April. Your clients will begin to expect it and look forward to it.
3. Remember to ask for referrals in your invitations.
4. Dinners are wonderful if you make them special. You can do this by planning them around a theme or in a special venue, such as a museum or botanical garden.
5. It's not about how much the event costs; it's about how you make your clients feel.
6. Do not talk business. The purpose of a client appreciation event is to celebrate your clients.
7. Avoid talking business with the referrals also.
8. Keep the focus on fun.
9. Do everything possible to make the event memorable. Hire a photographer.

10. The best events include food and an activity.
11. Invite your clients' family members.
12. Use unique invitations. Avoid the stock wedding-style invitation.
13. Provide a memorable gift, such as an inspirational book.
14. Don't be concerned about cost. Client appreciation is an investment you can count on.

Winning Client Appreciation Events

Here is a list of client appreciation events that have proven to be winners by financial advisors. Pick the events that both you and your clients will enjoy. You can conduct one major event, such as a picnic, and a few smaller ones, such as golf outings, each year.

1. Golf and tennis outings
2. Spectator sports and dinner: NFL football, Indy 500, Kentucky Derby, PGA golf tournaments, Stanley Cup Hockey finals
3. Ski Trips
4. Barbecues
5. Picnics
6. Chartered boat trips
7. Chartered local train trips
8. Opera
9. New Year's Party
10. Pig roast
11. Golf lessons with a professional
12. Putting tournament
13. Wine tasting
14. Bocci tournament
15. Broadway play
16. Spa getaway
17. Billiard tournament
18. Murder Mystery theater
19. Star gazing
20. Horseshoe tournament
21. Theme dinner party

22. Cooking lessons with a famous chef

23. The ballet

24. The symphony

25. Personal growth seminar with a well-known speaker

26. Ethnic dinners

27. Fishing trip

28. Fashion show

29. Private showing in a rented movie theater

30. Gardening clinics

31. Super Bowl party

32. Academy Award party

33. Rock and roll show

34. Birthday or anniversary party

35. Beach party

36. Skating party

37. Halloween party

38. Cigar and port social

39. Chartered bus to local historical or nature attraction

40. Bowling

Here are two resources that will provide you with the strategies and techniques you need for success with client events:

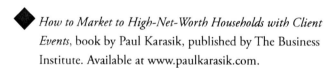 *How to Market to High-Net-Worth Households with Client Events*, book by Paul Karasik, published by The Business Institute. Available at www.paulkarasik.com.

How to Double Your Production with Client Events, a audio program by Paul Karasik, produced by The Business Institute. Available at www.paulkarasik.com.

PART THREE: THE PUBLIC SEMINAR

*Public seminars are the most popular
seminar style for financial professionals. Properly
implemented, public seminars can be very profitable.
They offer an easily controlled process for creating a
steady flow of qualified prospects.*

CHAPTER 8.
DETERMINING THE SIZE OF
YOUR PUBLIC SEMINAR

Before you begin the planning stage of your public seminar, you must decide what the final result will look like. How big would you like your seminar to be? There are three sizes to consider: the Living Room, the Club, and the Broadway Seminar. Each has its advantages and disadvantages.

The Living Room Seminar

This is a small seminar consisting of approximately ten to twenty-five participants or five to ten buying units, such as married couples.

Major advantages include simpler logistics and lower marketing costs. Living Room Seminars can be conducted in any small room – even in your living room, as the name suggests.

Small rooms, such as your office, the local library, community recreation rooms, and board rooms, are no-cost or low-cost venues and are easy to find and arrange. You can handle the planning, marketing, and implementation of Living Room Seminars alone or with the assistance of one person.

Small seminars are also an excellent choice if public speaking makes you feel uncomfortable. Giving a presentation to a small group is much less intimidating. If you do fear public speaking, the small group setting offers the perfect arena in which to learn to overcome your fear and develop your confidence.

> You can minimize your fear of speaking by delivering your presentation while you and your audience are seated around a large table. Your program will seem much more like a conversation than a presentation.

If you have a fear of public speaking and would like to overcome it, join Toastmasters International, an incredible organization with thousands of local chapters. Their strategies and techniques have helped countless people feel relaxed and even learn to enjoy presenting to groups. www.Toastmasters.org

The intimacy engendered by Living Room Seminars can be an advantage in developing rapport and building relationships with your participants. You will be able to address each person by name and create a more relaxed, informal atmosphere. Good eye contact in a small group will also enhance your relationship development.

The cost of marketing a small seminar is minimal. You can fill a room with ten or fifteen people for practically nothing, by telemarketing three or four hours a night over a one- or two-week period. Alternatively, a small, fairly inexpensive mailing of five hundred to one thousand letters can fill the seminar.

The obvious disadvantage of a small seminar is that the limited number of participants limits the potential for new business. But even though fewer people and fewer appointments means less business, it takes only one or two new clients to make the lowcost Living Room Seminar highly profitable.

The Club Seminar

This is a medium-size seminar, consisting of twenty-five to seventy-five participants, which is still small enough to allow for relationship building. It resembles a small nightclub setting.

Club Seminars provide you with twice the business potential of small seminars. And they are still fairly easy to implement with only minimal assistance; you won't need more than one person to help you at the seminar site.

The Club Seminar demands more in terms of resources. This size seminar requires a more substantial investment of time for planning and money for marketing. The added cost of marketing creates an element of risk if the marketing is ineffective and attendance is poor.

Presentations at Club Seminars maintain many of the advantages of small seminars. You will be available for personal contact with participants before and after your program, and good eye contact is easy during the program. If you are uncomfortable making presentations, you will find Club Seminars somewhat more intimidating than Living Room Seminars but still small enough to feel conversational rather than formal.

The most significant advantage of the Club Seminar is the efficiency of the system. If you systematize your seminar marketing process, you will limit your investment of time. The small and medium seminars both require the same amount of your time to deliver. But the Club Seminar yields approximately twice the results.

The medium seminar demands a larger venue, such as a restaurant or hotel meeting room. These sites require more lead time to reserve. If you plan to serve food, you might have to commit to a minimum number of meals.

Marketing by telephone will require two or three callers for about two weeks before the event, which means added expense and availability of telephone stations. Direct mail will also require a more substantial investment. If you intend to fill the room with fifty people, you will have to mail twenty-five hundred to five thousand invitations, which will add more to your cost.

> One of the best ways to improve efficiency is to use a multiple-day strategy. In other words, use one marketing campaign but offer the same program on two or three different days. This will keep your groups small and more conducive to forming relationships.

The Broadway Seminar

This is a large seminar consisting of more than fifty people. It offers financial advisors the opportunity to present to a large group of people and thereby leverage the investment of up-front seminar time.

The Broadway Seminar works especially well if you share the event with other financial advisors. The time and resources for implementing the seminar and the appointments that result from it can all be shared.

The large seminar approach also works well if you present a specific investment product idea. In this case, your purpose would be to sell a product rather than sell the relationship. If you enjoy the performance aspect of leading seminars, you will find the Broadway Seminar most satisfying.

The Broadway Seminar has a few significant disadvantages. As the name suggests, this seminar can be a major production. It requires a minimum of three people at the seminar site to handle the room setup, sign-in activities, on-site appointment setting, and other tasks.

The cost and time associated with marketing the Broadway Seminar adds an increased level of risk. More dollars will be needed for the room, marketing, and perhaps staff. More time will be needed for planning and marketing.

But the biggest drawback of the large seminar is the lack of time to create and build relationships. You will not have enough time to talk to many participants before or after the program.

CHAPTER 9.
CHOOSING YOUR MARKETING STRATEGY

You may choose from the four effective methods for marketing your public seminar: direct mail, telemarketing, direct mail combined with telemarketing, and advertising. Use the following criteria to decide which marketing strategy is best for you.

Your staff

If you are a one-person shop, you can easily outsource direct mail. If, on the other hand, you work in a larger office that has a few phone stations and part-time telephone people, telemarketing might work well. If you live in or near a college town, the availability of part-time telephone people helps to make telemarketing a viable choice.

Your office set-up

If you have a large office with a few phone stations that can be used during the early evening hours, the telephone might be an important consideration.

Your personal style

If you prefer not to be involved with training or management responsibilities, direct mail and advertising are better choices.

Your budget

If you are new to the business or have limited marketing funds, the telephone is perfect for marketing Living Room Seminars by yourself with practically no financial investment.

Your geographic area

In metropolitan areas, advertising can be expensive and not as targeted as direct mail. But in a resort community, advertising in the local rag can be an inexpensive and effective strategy for filling up your seminar room.

Direct mail is usually the most cost-effective strategy, but it is worth your time to conduct informal research with two great sources: colleagues and wholesalers. Ask what has worked best to fill seats at their seminars: advertising, telephone, or direct mail. If they say nothing worked, most likely they implemented the strategy incorrectly; they may have tried to sell a poor topic or used bad mailing lists or ineffective invitations.

> Network at one of your professional associations. Attend a local chapter meeting of the Financial Planning Association or the National Association of Insurance and Financial Advisors, and speak to people who regularly conducts seminars in your area about their marketing methods. It's always best to learn from other people's experience.

CHAPTER 10.
THE ART AND SCIENCE OF
DIRECT MAIL MARKETING

Direct mail marketing is the most common strategy for promoting financial seminars. Although it has become more costly in recent years because of rising postal rates, direct mail can be targeted, and it is easy to implement.

Testing the List

Countless variables exist in direct mail marketing, and there is only one way to determine the best choice in any situation: test one variable against another. The fundamental method for testing any element in direct mail promotion is the A/B split. A computer command divides the mailing list in half, assigning all the even-numbered names to the "A" list and all the odd-numbered names to the "B" list. Two different mailings are then sent out, one to the "A" list and one to the "B" list, and the results are compared.

For example, to test the response to two different versions of your invitation copy, you would send one version to the "A" list and the other version to the "B" list. Based on the response you received, and assuming there were no other variables, you would know which copy works better.

Ten response factors that can be tested include:

1. The list
2. Invitation style
3. Invitation copy
4. Location
5. Day

6. Time
7. Bulk mail versus first class
8. Mail permit versus stamp
9. Multiple mailing
10. Food or no food

The Five Components of Direct Mail Marketing

1. The list. Who will receive your invitations? The names on your mailing list will have a major impact on both the quality and quantity of the response you receive.
2. Copy and design. What does your invitation say and how does it look? You need persuasive copy and an effective layout.
3. The invitation package. What form does your invitation take, and what else do you include in the envelope besides the invitation?
4. Printing and assembling.
5. Mailing.

Let's look at each element in more detail.

The List

You can purchase mailing lists by zip code, income, age, profession, gender, or other factors. It is important to ask your list supplier when the list was cleaned or updated. Dirty lists will cost you money in undeliverable mail and will lower the response rate.

> You can easily find out how clean the list is by sending out a test mailing using first-class mail. Count the number of returned pieces and use that number to calculate the average percentage of outdated names.

Maps with Zip Codes. Most lists for financial seminars are chosen by zip code, so it's handy to have maps with zip codes.

The following companies specialize in targeted consumer lists. You can get mailing labels in any form you like. In most cases, phone numbers are also available.

 www.Dunhills.com
www.infoUSA.com
www.ALC.com

Building your own in-house mailing list may be even more important than buying lists. Your own list can be extremely lucrative. Be sure to include the following people on your own list:

Inquirers. Every time someone calls you or responds to any lead generation program, put that person on your mailing list. Collect names and addresses whenever possible. For example, if you give other talks, such as at a local Rotary meeting or for your church group, collect names and add them to your list.

No-shows. Add to your mailing list for future programs anyone who signed up to attend a seminar but did not show. Many of these people will eventually respond and attend one of your programs.

Seminar alumni. Add all participants of your seminars to your mailing list. If they haven't taken advantage of your consultation, your mailings will remind them of your availability. They also might decide to attend a future seminar, and you will have another opportunity to set an appointment with them. It is not unusual for some people to move slowly and finally make a decision to move ahead with you after repeated exposure.

Client referrals. Whether you meet these referrals at seminars or simply get their names from your clients, add them to your mailing list.

Your clients' CPAs. Ask your clients for the names of their CPAs and add them to your in-house mailing list.

Copy and Design

Your invitation must be written and designed in a compelling manner that will attract participants to your seminar.

The design of your seminar invitation should include graphic considerations whenever possible. Simple additions, such as your photo or seminar site logo, will add to the invitation's appeal. Breaking up the copy with elements such as bold type, italics, a different typeface, white space, and bullets will also enhance the effectiveness of your invitation.

If you write your own copy, consider the following simple guidelines.

Focus on benefits. People will attend your seminar to gain rewards or avoid punishment. Education is a feature, and you must include what they will learn in your content; but the benefits provide the compelling reasons for them to attend. For example, will your participants save money, enjoy their money more, or manage their money more effectively? Emphasize these benefits. Don't hesitate to repeat the benefits or paraphrase them a few times.

Use short sentences, phrases, and paragraphs. Good copy is always easy to read and understand. Generally, keeping your sentences and paragraphs short will help you communicate more effectively. Bulleted items are effective tools for writing copy because they are short by definition.

Use powerful, direct language. An invitation is basically a sales piece designed to close on an action. The size of your invitation limits the number of words you may use; therefore you must maximize their power.

Here are twenty-two power phrases you can choose from for your seminar invitation.

1. Isn't it time you . . .
2. Take this important first step.
3. There has never been a better time to . . .
4. You owe it to yourself and your family to . . .
5. This program will give you a new perspective on . . .
6. It's no secret that financial planning is . . .
7. Confused about . . .
8. Will you be ready for . . .
9. What's the most effective way to . . .
10. Have you ever wished . . .
11. Today, more than ever . . .
12. It's never too late to . . .
13. As a financial advisor who specializes in . . .
14. You'll never have to worry about . . .
15. Before investing your money, you should invest your time . . .
16. You'll be in control when you . . .

17. You've got an important decision to make.
18. Don't miss this opportunity to learn . . .
19. This seminar is an investment in your future.
20. Planning often makes the difference between success and failure.
21. If you're like most people, you probably . . .
22. You'll discover how easy it is to . . .

An effective seminar invitation contains several universal modules. It's easy to overlook information that can affect the response you receive. Use the following checklist when you design your invitation and write your copy.

[ ] Headline. A opening statement or question – a grabber – is an effective way to begin an invitation. The purpose of the grabber is to attract attention, gain involvement, and encourage readers to read on.

[ ] Who should attend. Is your program for pre-retirees? Women? Young married couples? Investors? Seniors?

[ ] Benefit. Avoid getting bogged down in features. Benefits, what the seminar will do for participants, is more important to them than what they will learn.

[ ] What they will learn. What specific topics will you cover?

[ ] Date, time, place. This information should be displayed so it is easy to read. Pull out the copy and let it stand alone when possible.

[ ] Your biography. Include your qualifications for speaking on the subject, such as years in the business, education, professional designations.

[ ] Your photo. A photo can help the participants get to know you a little before they even attend the seminar.

[ ] Guest speaker. Include information about any guest speakers and, if possible, their photos.

[ ] Directions. If necessary, include directions to the seminar site.

[ ] Agenda. If the event consists of different parts, list them. For example:

6:00 p.m. to 6:30 p.m. Wine and Cheese
6:30 p.m. to 7:30 p.m. Dinner
7:30 p.m. to 8:30 p.m. Seminar

[ ] What materials will be included. Will you be giving out a workbook, book, report, or tip sheet? This will add value to the seminar and help attract more participants.

[ ] Food or drink. If you are providing a free meal or refreshments, be sure to include this information prominently.

> If you conduct your seminar at a well-known restaurant or site, include the logo of the event site on your invitation.

[ ] How to register. Make this information stand out. Give a phone number to call or tell what should be mailed in and where. Use a toll free number if possible.

[ ] Free. Most likely your seminar is free. This is still one of the most loved words in the English language. Emphasize this word with bold type, all caps, or a slightly larger font.

> Print "Seminar Invitation Enclosed" on the envelope. It will increase your response rate.

> For effective invitation copy that you can customize for your seminar, see MD 5. Public Seminar Invitation Copy, in Chapter 19. You can adapt the copy for any of the common seminar invitation styles.

Be sure to secure approval from your compliance department for all of your seminar components.

The Invitation Package

Your invitation package can consist of one or more elements. Additional elements add expense, but they also result in a better response to your mailing. The three most common elements of an invitation package are the invitation itself, the reply card, and tickets.

The invitation. This describes the seminar and gives important information, such as the topic, date, time, and place. Three styles are the most popular and most effective for seminar invitations: letter, greeting card, and wedding.

Each of these styles has many variations to choose from. Wedding style invitations come in different sizes, shapes, paper, and so forth. Letter style can be the standard letter format, letters in window envelopes, or multipage letters. Greeting card style invitations are available in different colors and with a choice of graphics.

It is difficult to say which style is more effective. Although most vendors will tout one over the other, the only sure way to know is to test.

Post-paid reply postcard. You can purchase a permit number from your local post office. It takes approximately four days to get your number. The post-paid reply card makes it easier for people to register and increases your response rate.

 See MD 6. Post-Paid Reply Postcard, in Chapter19.

Tickets. Enclosing four tickets, each admitting two adults to your seminar, will add value to the event. You can also print the date, time, location, and your toll free number on the back to provide a reminder of the details.

 See MD 7. Public Seminar Tickets, in Chapter 19.

Remember: It's the results that count. The best way to decide which invitation package is right for you is to test a few different styles and contents, and measure the results. More costly invitation packages do not necessarily produce better results.

Printing and Assembling

After you have written your copy and designed your invitation package, you will need to print the invitations and have them assembled for mailing.

You can assemble the invitation packages yourself or let the printer do it. It is usually more efficient to outsource this task. Most printers are equipped to prepare your invitation packages for labels and mailing.

Here are a few tips and guidelines for choosing a printer.

1. Check with local printers first. You will probably save time and ship-

ping costs by having your invitation package printed locally.

2. Find out what types of printing they specialize in. Most printers are equipped for certain types of printing, such as color brochures, books, or direct mail. It would be helpful if the printer you choose has experience with direct mail printing. The suitability of the printer for your particular job will dramatically affect your cost.

3. Ask for a delivery schedule. Late delivery can destroy your marketing schedule and ruin your seminar marketing efforts.

4. Search the Internet. You might find some exceptional deals. Printing can be purchased very effectively online, and sometimes the pricing makes it an excellent option. Be sure to factor in shipping costs.

5. Get multiple quotes. Shop around for at least three quotes before choosing a printer.

Mailing

The mailing process involves putting the labels or addresses and postage on the invitations and delivering them to the post office. You can choose to do this yourself or use a local mailing service.

You must decide how you will mail your invitation package and how you will apply the postage. Bulk mail is less expensive than first class but generally takes five to ten days longer to arrive. The good news is that bulk mail has been found to be as effective as firstclass mail in terms of response.

Assuming you have planned your direct mail campaign well and can afford the time to use bulk mail, the only advantage of first class is that undeliverable mail will be returned to you. That will tell you how clean your list is and give you the opportunity to update it.

You need a permit to qualify for bulk mail reduced rates. The mail must be bundled according to post office regulations. Postage can be applied with a stamp or printed directly on the envelope.

Inquire at your local post office for cost and how to prepare or bundle your mail to meet the requirements for the reduced rates. You can also check out the United States Postal Service's excellent Web site.

 United States Postal Service www.usps.com

Many companies offer both printing and mailing services. Some printing companies work as a team with a mailing service. Each knows the other's system, and the process can be seamless.

It is usually best to outsource the mailing process because it is time consuming; if you choose to do it yourself, you will most likely need to hire at least one person to help you, and the savings will be negligible.

The Turn-Key Marketing Solution. Using a one-stop vendor who handles every aspect of direct mail promotion is a practical and highly efficient way to fill the seats at your seminar.

These marketing companies specialize in filling seats at financial seminars. They provide the list; write the copy; create the invitation package; and print, assemble, and mail the invitation.

You can save some money by purchasing each item separately, but it is much more efficient to outsource the work to a competent direct mail service that can take care of filling the seats.

If you intend to market your seminars on an ongoing basis, the one-stop companies will streamline your process and allow you and your organization to concentrate on your most important activities: delivering seminars, meeting prospects, and obtaining new business.

Some of these turn-key companies provide additional services. They may offer toll free lines for taking reservations, mail confirmation letters, telephone confirmations, and telemarket to the mailing list to improve the response rate. Ask about the availability of these services. Interview each company to get price quotes and to determine which is the best fit for your needs.

★ Turn-Key Marketing Services
    www.cismarketing.com
    www.seminardirect.com
    www.financialseminarservices.com
    www.seminarinnovations.com

CHAPTER 11.
THE DIRECT MAIL SUCCESS PLAN

Your success plan begins approximately eight weeks before your seminar. Keep in mind that as you become more experienced and systematized, you will be able to reduce the time needed to market your seminar considerably.

It is much better to complete the seminar marketing steps needed for a successful direct mail campaign with time to spare than to lose participation because of poor planning and implementation.

8 Weeks before the Event
[ ] Step 1. Select and book the event location.
[ ] Step 2. Assemble your mailing list.
[ ] Step 3. Produce your invitation package.

6 Weeks before the Event
[ ] Step 4. Prepare your seminar workbooks and materials.

4 Weeks before the Event
[ ] Step 5. Prepare your presentation.
[ ] Step 6. Arrange your audiovisual needs.
[ ] Step 7. Mail your invitation packages.

3 Weeks before the Event
[ ] Step 8. Begin taking reservations and mailing confirmations.

2 Weeks before the Event
[ ] Step 9. Confirm participants a second time by phone.

1 Week before the Event
[ ] Step 10. Review and rehearse your presentation.
[ ] Step 11. Confirm seminar details.

The Day before the Event
[ ] Step 12. Confirm participants again, and confirm the final count with the site.

Step 1. Select and book the event location.
This step includes choosing and booking the appropriate seminar site and deciding on the day, date, and time.

Choose the best site. Before you can do that, you must decide if you will serve a meal, just refreshments, or nothing. The most significant advantage of serving a meal is that you will fill more seats at your seminar by offering a free meal. Most turn-key seminar marketing companies recommend that you offer a meal. They know your results will improve markedly.

Because a percentage of participants attend just for the meal, the quality of participants will be degraded somewhat. The meal also adds expense to your seminar. And it affects how you are perceived. If your restaurant and food offering is second tier, you might attract fewer affluent prospects.

Obviously you will save money by not serving a meal, but this should not be the determining factor. The most significant reason for not serving food is to attract a more qualified audience. Fewer people might attend the event, but the quality of attendees will be higher. Those who do attend your seminar will be there to hear what you have to say.

Filling more seats should not be the primary reason for serving food. The guideline should be the potential for more appointments and more new business. Always calculate your return on investment. The only way to know for sure if serving a meal is right for you is to test, and calculate the response. Use this number to help you make your decision.

After you have decided about the meal, you can begin collecting ideas for the seminar site. Consider the following six criteria when choosing your site:

1. Convenience. The best seminar site is within a fifteen- to twenty-minute drive of your target market.
2. Parking. Ample parking, with good access to the door, makes it easy for your participants.
3. Privacy. The function room needs to be free from distractions.
4. Size. If you conduct small seminars, do not use large rooms that will feel empty.
5. Image. Choose a site that your target market will feel comfortable in. If you target the affluent, select an upscale venue.
6. Access. Be sure you have access to the room at least one hour prior to the start of your event. You will need preparation time.

> Scan the event section in your local newspapers to see where others hold their seminars. You may discover an excellent site you would not have thought of otherwise.

If you will not serve meals, consider holding your event in a library, community recreation room, your office, or even your home, if it is big enough. If you will serve meals or refreshments, your best locations will be restaurants, hotels, and country clubs. Of these, restaurants and county clubs usually attract the most response. If you plan large seminars, hotels are the best choice.

Choose the best day. The best days for seminars are Tuesday, Wednesday, Thursday, and Saturday. These days attract the best responses.

Most advisors fail to realize the convenience of Saturdays for many people. Smallbusiness owners, a prime target market for many advisors, are much more likely to attend your seminar on a Saturday morning, when they are free of their business responsibilities.

Avoid choosing days that conflict with holidays, national and local events, and popular sporting events, such as playoffs or the World Series.

Choose the best time. The best time for your seminar will depend on whether you intend to serve food.

If you plan to serve a meal, certain times are most effective. You can adapt the times given below to fit the length of your seminar, local traffic patterns, your target market, and any other pertinent factors.

An effective schedule for a breakfast seminar
8:30 a.m. – Doors open
9:00 a.m. – Breakfast served
9:30 a.m. – Seminar begins

An effective schedule for a lunch seminar
10:00 a.m. – Doors open
10:30 a.m. – Seminar begins
12:00 p.m. – Lunch served

An effective schedule for a dinner seminar
5:00 p.m. – Doors open
5:30 p.m. – Seminar begins
7:00 p.m. – Dinner served

Morning and evening are the best times for seminars at which only light refreshments are served.

Morning
9:30 a.m. – Doors open
10:00 a.m. to 11:30 a.m. – Seminar

Evening
6:30 p.m. – Doors open
7:00 p.m. to 8:30 p.m. – Seminar

Step 2. Assemble your mailing list.
The best seminar mailing list is a combination of a purchased list and a list you continually build in house. Follow the guidelines for mailing lists outlined in

Chapter 10. Print out the labels from your in-house list, or work with your vendor to merge your inhouse list with the purchased mailing list.

Step 3. Produce your invitation package.
Customize the copy provided in this manual or write your own copy, work with your vendors to perfect it, and solicit feedback from lots of people before you finalize it.

> Always ask for feedback from people who know nothing about your business. Ask friends who might be part of your target market for feedback. Their inexperienced eyes will often see things from a fresh and creative viewpoint.

Don't be surprised if things go more slowly than you planned. When you work as a team with your own staff, outside assistants, and vendors, this inherently adds time to the process. Expect delays. Once you have systematized your seminar process, you will be able to complete this step in half the time.

Step 4. Prepare your seminar workbooks and materials.
If you plan to use workbooks, allow enough time to order them. If you will distribute company brochures, you might need to order them also. Other materials you might want to prepare include books, article reprints, tip sheets, other information sheets, and customized folders to hold your seminar handouts.

Step 5. Prepare your presentation.
Allow yourself enough time to review your presentation and customize it to fit you and your style. Review each slide, add slides if necessary, and make adjustments to fit your target audience. This step will take more time and be more relevant the first few times you present your seminar.

Step 6. Arrange your audiovisual needs.
You will need to arrange your audiovisual needs in advance to allow enough time to purchase or rent equipment if necessary.

You will need a laptop computer, projector, and screen for your PowerPoint slides. You might want to use a flip chart for interactive exercises, and you will need a microphone and sound system if you have more than twenty-five participants.

First check with your seminar facility. Many restaurants, hotels, and country clubs will let you use the house sound system at no extra charge. Check with them before making other arrangements. You will need to provide the microphone.

The best microphone for seminars is a wireless lavalier that clips onto your shirt or lapel. It is simple to set up and operate. It allows you freedom of movement and leaves your hands free. If you intend to present regularly to medium and large groups, it will be a worthwhile purchase, since even a few rentals will cost more than buying it.

You will need to decide whether you want to rent or purchase a projector and screen if you don't already own them. Some sites provide a screen free of charge.

Step 7. Mail your invitation packages.
Your invitation packages need to be mailed one month before the seminar to allow them to arrive approximately three weeks before the event. Bulk mail will arrive two and one-half to three weeks before the event, which is good lead time, and first class will arrive a few days earlier.

Step 8. Begin taking reservations and mailing confirmations.
Participants will begin making reservations approximately a week after your mail is dropped. Before they start, you need to make arrangements for taking phone messages.

If you decide to take the reservations at your office, set up a phone with a toll free number. This gives you a more professional image. Your telephone company can assign a toll free number to a local number. Ideally you should take reservations live. If that's not always possible, use a voice-mail service or a combination of the two.

The alternative to setting up your own toll free number with voice mail is to use a service that specializes in taking reservations for seminars. Most of the seminar mailing companies can take your reservations with a live attendant 24-7. These services can also make confirmation calls.

If you receive reservations by telephone, be sure to have your phone answered in a professional way. Provide your staff or your phone service with a customized script.

This first contact can be extremely valuable in qualifying your participants. Ask for permission to ask questions, and then gather information that you can store in your contact management system.

When you receive registrations by mail, you can call the registrants, thank them for registering, and gather information that will be helpful in qualifying them and building a relationship.

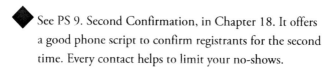 See PS 8. Taking a Reservation, in Chapter 18. It is an effective phone script you can customize for your company and seminar. This script will help you to initiate the relationship and qualify the registrant. Questions in the script will enable you to determine if your participant is a do-it-yourselfer or a delegator when it comes to financial planning. You can add or delete questions depending on your products or services.

Step 9. Confirm participants a second time by phone.
This phone call will give you the opportunity to build trust and rapport.

See PS 9. Second Confirmation, in Chapter 18. It offers a good phone script to confirm registrants for the second time. Every contact helps to limit your no-shows.

Step 10. Review and rehearse your presentation.
As the seminar nears, you need to go through your slides and script so that you feel comfortable with the material. It helps to present your seminar once or twice to a friendly audience of friends or associates.

Step 11. Confirm seminar details.
Confirm all the details with enough time to spare in case you need to make corrections or improvements. Confirm the following:

a. Audio visual equipment

b. Guest speaker

c. Event room

d. Staff arrangements

e. Food service

Step 12. Confirm participants again, and confirm the final count with the site.
Your final confirmation telephone call should be made in the evening of the day
before your event. If you fail to reach the registrant the night before, and you
have daytime numbers, you can call on the day of the event. The rule here is to
call within approximately twenty-four hours of the seminar.

◆ Use PS 10, the phone script for Final Confirmation,
found in Chapter 18. If you still haven't asked the qualifying questions contained in PS 8, do it during this final
phone contact.

CHAPTER 12.
THE ART AND SCIENCE OF
TELEMARKETING YOUR
SEMINAR

Telemarketing is an excellent strategy for filling the seats at your seminar. It's one of the most cost-effective methods.

Advantages of Telemarketing

1. You can work with a relatively short lead time. For example, you can fill the seats of your seminar in two weeks or less.
2. Assuming you will be phoning in a local area, the telephone is a cost-effective approach to marketing your seminar. Your primary expense will be the salary of the telemarketers.
3. The telephone provides you with the opportunity to begin to build rapport with your seminar participants.

Disadvantages of Telemarketing

1. You will need to hire, train, and manage the telemarketers or find the right experienced person to do it for you. If you have never used the telephone to promote or sell, you might have some difficulty with this process.
2. Telemarketing entails logistical challenges. You will need at least two – and preferably three or four – telephones available. If your office is not equipped or phones are not available, telephone promotion could become too costly.

3. Probably the biggest disadvantage is a recent development: a new federal law that established the do-not-call list. People can request that their names and phone numbers be placed on this list. Telemarketers must not call these households; if they do, they risk severe fines.

Millions of households have already requested placement on the do-not-call list. This will increase the frequency of calls to households not on the list, which in turn will motivate those households to go on the list. It is advisable to use caution and avoid breaking any laws.

The Components of Telemarketing

The telemarketing process involves three components: location, staffing, and script and calling procedures.

Location. You have two choices for the location of your telemarketing program: callers may work in your office or from home. The advantage of having them work in your office is that you can have direct supervision over them: calls can be monitored, questions can be answered quickly, and coaching can be provided. The disadvantage is that you will need to provide space and telephones, and you or an assistant will need to supervise the callers.

A practical alternative is to hire callers and allow them to work from their homes. The calls will be local, so they will not incur any telephone charges. Provide your callers with the call list and have them fill out call tracking sheets similar to the one described later in this chapter.

Staffing. You may secure your telemarketers through a temp agency or by finding them yourself. If a temp agency can provide you with experienced callers, you will certainly be ahead of the game. You will have streamlined your task list. The temp agency will also take care of all the paperwork associated with employees.

If you cannot locate a temp agency, the next best choice is to find a source you can rely on for a steady supply of qualified workers. A nearby college, for example, is a good source. You can list your needs with the college or on bulletin boards. If you can find a few good people, there is a good chance you can keep them for a year or more. You can also ask them to recruit their friends and acquaintances.

One of the most efficient methods is the internet. Go to www.craigslist.org and for a few dollars you can place an add that will generate quite a few candidates for you to interview. There is no perfect copy for a help-wanted advertisement. Here is some copy you might want to begin with:

> Make Big Money on the Telephone. No Selling. Part-
> time. Must be positive, energetic, and have a good phone
> voice. Call 777-7777. Ask for Stuart.

Plan to pay your callers a base salary plus a commission for each person they recruit for the seminar. By using a base salary plus commission for actual attendance at the seminar, you will encourage your telemarketers to keep the ultimate objective in mind and minimize no-shows.

The most exciting part of using telemarketing as a promotional strategy is the predictability of positive results. There is no way of knowing your exact results, but you will achieve success. Here is the golden rule for success regarding telephone marketing of any kind: One thing I know, and I know it well. The more calls I make, the more I sell.

If you find a telephone person who is talented, enjoys phone work, and fits into your office culture, you might want to offer her or him the responsibility of interviewing, training, and managing callers and the entire telemarketing operation.

You can expect the following results per caller:

25 to 50 calls per hour
5 to 10 contacts per hour who ask for invitations
1 registrant who will show up at the seminar per hour of calling

In other words, in a three-hour calling session, each caller will enroll three participants in your seminar.

Script and calling procedures. There is no perfect script for telemarketing, but four modules must be included:
  1. An introduction of yourself and your company
  2. The reason you are calling
  3. What's in it for them
  4. A call for action

◆ PS 11, found in Chapter 18, is a basic phone script that will work well. Keep the benefits and four modules in place, and adapt it to your style.

A script should never be read. It is merely a format, an outline listing key points the caller must cover during the conversation. Callers should be trained to sound conversational; a warm friendly voice will always achieve better results than a voice that is merely reading a script.

Give your callers permission to customize your script. Let the callers adapt the script to their own styles and add or delete words to make the script come alive.

After using a script for a few hours, callers should be able to work without referring to it. Experienced callers will quickly be able to work from a few notes containing logistical information, such as the topic, time, date, and place of the event.

The Best Time to Make Calls

The best time to call residences is in the early evening. The exact times will vary according to your target audience and geographical location. In general, the best time to phone is between 4:00 p.m. and 9:00 p.m. on weekdays. Another great time to phone is Sunday evening during the same hours, when practically everyone is home.

Daily Tracking Sheets

Callers must keep daily records of their work. These essential records enable you to refine your promotion techniques, improve your efficiency, and evaluate the effectiveness of each caller.

On tracking sheets similar to

 MD 20. Call Tracking Sheet, found in Chapter 19

each caller puts a hash mark after each call, contact, and commitment. A commitment is made when the contact says he or she wants to attend and an invitation is sent out for confirmation. Each caller keeps a separate tracking sheet for each calling session. And each caller should keep a list of the people who have made a commitment to attend.

Of course at the seminar itself, you record the names of the people who actually do attend. From that list you determine the financial bonuses callers receive for their contacts who did show up. In addition, you can give a prize to the caller who had the most attendees from his or her list of committed contacts.

Creating a Telephone Seminar Marketing Machine

Ideally, you will promote seminars regularly. The advantage of repeated promotion is that it builds momentum. As with any form of marketing, repeated telephone exposure produces a snowball effect. You'll be amazed at how an individual can be a no-show three times, finally attend one of your seminars, and eventually become a client. As with any form of sales, you must be willing to ask for the order more than once.

After each seminar, place your no-shows on a list and continue to call to invite them to upcoming seminars. Also, email your schedule of upcoming seminars to no-shows, past participants, and current clients.

Here are the steps to follow to conduct successful telemarketing campaigns for your seminars. Details for implementing Step 2 are in this chapter; details for the other steps can be found in Chapters 10 and 11.

8 Weeks before the Event
[ ] Step 1. Select and book the event location.
[ ] Step 2. Hire telemarketing staff. You will need about two weeks to interview and hire callers.
[ ] Step 3. Produce your invitation package.

6 Weeks before the Event
[ ] Step 4. Prepare your seminar workbooks and materials.

4 Weeks before the Event
[ ] Step 5. Begin calling. It will take three to four weeks to secure one hundred participants. If your objective is fifty participants, it will take about two weeks, using three callers part-time Sunday through Thurs-

day.

[ ] Step 6. Prepare your presentation.

[ ] Step 7. Arrange your audio-visual needs.

2 Weeks before the Event

[ ] Step 8. Confirm participants a second time by phone. This is the time to qualify the registrants and gather information. Use PS 9, the phone script for Second Confirmation.

1 Week before the Event

[ ] Step 9. Review and rehearse your presentation.

[ ] Step 10. Confirm seminar details.

The Day before the event

[ ] Step 11. Confirm participants again, and confirm the final count with the site. Use PS 10, the phone script for Final Confirmation.

CHAPTER 13.
THE ADVERTISING SUCCESS PLAN

Advertising your seminar is the least effective strategy, but it can work in certain circumstances. When you use the media as a tool for public relations or free publicity, it can also fill additional seats.

The biggest drawback of most advertising is lack of targeting and cost. Advertising exposes only a small percentage of your target market to your message. You can minimize this obstacle through repetition. But in doing so, your investment climbs, making advertising a poor promotion choice.

Newspapers

Of the media choices, the newspaper is the most effective for seminar marketing. If you decide to run an advertisement, follow these guidelines:

1. Run your ad on Sundays and Tuesdays, the best days to advertise.
2. Avoid advertising on Friday.
3. Do not advertise the day the grocery ads appear.
4. To save money, advertise in local editions of big newspapers.
5. Always use a headline in your ad to attract attention.
6. Stress the benefits of the seminar.
7. Make the copy simple and easy to read.
8. Keep your sentences and paragraphs short.
9. Use adequate white space.
10. Include your photo.
11. Employ graphics when possible.

12. Mention anything free, like refreshments or workbooks.

13. Business and finance sections work the best.

14. The front of the section is best.

15. The best page location is the upper right.

16. Multiple exposures increase your response rates.

17. Larger ads get a better response.

18. Include a strong call to action.

19. Identify yourself with a logo.

20. Use a toll free number for registrations.

 MD 9. Newspaper Advertisement or Insert, in Chapter 19, gives you copy for an advertisement that you can customize with your title, photo, bio, logo, graphics, and other details.

The Two Most Successful Newspaper Strategies

The two most effective strategies for using newspapers involve small community papers.

Advertisements work reasonably well in the weekly newspapers available in small communities. The response is often good in relation to the cost. These weekly newspapers are usually less crowded with advertisements, and your advertisement will stand out more.

Weekly newspapers in vacation areas, usually available for free, will perform excellently. If you live in or near a vacation spot, this can be an easy and inexpensive way to fill the seats at your seminar.

The second excellent strategy for advertising with newspapers involves the 8 6" x 11" flyers inserted in small community papers, whether weeklies or dailies. The cost is usually low enough to make it feasible, and the response should be high enough to fill seats at your seminar.

Expand the size of your newspaper advertisement and

use it as a flyer. Add graphics such as your company logo, your photo, or appropriate artwork.

◆ See MD 9. Newspaper Advertisement or Insert, in Chapter 19.

⚡ Use both the advertisement and the flyer. Put the insert in the newspaper two weeks before the seminar, and run the advertisement one week before the seminar.

How to Fill Seats with Free Promotion

One of the easiest ways to fill seats is to harness the power of the free calendar announcement. Almost all newspapers offer their readers a list of local current events, and the listings are almost always free. The same is usually true for chamber of commerce newsletters; many offer free listings for members.

First, identify newspapers that your target audience is likely to read, and find out if they publish a calendar of events. Call each paper to identify the contact person for placing a calendar announcement. Ask about the preferred method for submitting information (mail, fax, e-mail) and find out the deadline. Keep a list of the deadlines, and submit your announcement in a timely fashion.

Whenever you work with the media, it is important to stay in touch with the contact person. Once you establish a relationship, there is an excellent chance you will be able to list all future events.

Social Media Marketing

Social media such as LinkedIn and Facebook provide opportunities for promoting your seminar and getting the word out. The big issue is compliance. It is essential to confer with your compliance department.

◆ Here are two good resources to get you up to speed with social media marketing. *The Social Advisor: Social Media Marketing for the Financial Services Industry*, by McIllwain, Malone and Smith *The Social Media Handbook for financial Advisors*, by Halloran, Thies, and Cates

To increase the likelihood of receiving this free newspaper coverage, submit your information in a professional manner. Follow these guidelines for producing your calendar announcement:

1. Double-space your copy on your letterhead.
2. Provide a release date.
3. Include a contact name and telephone number.
4. Be direct. List who, what, where, when, and why.
5. Keep it short.
6. Follow up with a phone call.

 See Chapter 19 for MD 11. Sample Calendar Announcement.

Radio and Television

Broadcast media, radio and television, have not proven to be cost effective for seminar advertising. They are expensive, particularly during the hours in which you would most want your ad to be aired.

The best strategy for using broadcast media involves teaming up with the host of a local finance show. You can offer the host a fee to appear at your seminar and also pay for the advertising. The host might also have a mailing list that you could use.

Be sure to get all arrangements in writing. Your letter of agreement should include:

- financial arrangements and payment schedule
- responsibilities of the speaker
- your responsibilities
- cancellations rights and penalties

PART FOUR: THE IN-HOUSE SEMINAR

*Opportunities to present sponsored or in-house seminars are
practically unlimited. Many organizations offer these opportunities
and will promote you to members of their group. You don't have to spend
the time or incur the expenses associated with filling public
seminars. All you have to do is show up.*

The outstanding difference between in-house seminars and all others is that
you must adjust content and format to meet the needs of the group. For example, you may be offered many opportunities for short speaking engagements
rather than for the longer seminar format. This will require an investment of
preparation time.

As mentioned in Chapter 2, organizations that may offer the opportunity
to present your program to their membership include:

1. professional and trade associations
2. adult and continuing education programs
3. service and fraternal organizations
4. church and religious groups
5. corporate programs
6. nonprofit organizations
7. senior centers and senior living communities

CHAPTER 14. MEDIA KITS: THE SECRET TO BOOKING IN-HOUSE SEMINARS FAST

The secret to booking in-house seminars fast is to assemble a media kit that positions you as an experienced and professional presenter. It is not costly to create an impressive media kit.

The Elements of a Media Kit

A complete media kit consists of eleven elements. You may already have some of these elements; others you might have to develop. Put together as many as you can right now, and add the rest in time. Your media kit will get you in the door of an organization and lead to many lucrative in-house opportunities.

Element One: The Cover letter. This is a letter that will remind decision makers of your telephone conversation and give them all of the relevant contact information. Keep the letter short. You want them to focus on your material, not the cover letter.

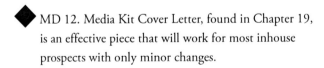 MD 12. Media Kit Cover Letter, found in Chapter 19, is an effective piece that will work for most inhouse prospects with only minor changes.

Element Two: The Presentation Description. This can be a simple, single sheet giving the title, program description, topics covered, benefits, and what the audience will learn.

◆ You can customize MD 13. In-House Program Description, a sample program description found in Chapter 19, to your target audience.

Element Three: The Company Brochure. If you have a company brochure describing your firm and what you do, be sure to include it.

Element Four: The Bio. A bio is different from a resumé. Your bio positions you to speak on this topic and to this group. Your bio should answer these questions: Why should we ask this person to speak to our group? What will this presentation mean to our members? A good bio should be narrative in style. Include only the facts that reinforce your competence to speak on this subject to this audience, such as your professional designations.

Element Five: The Photo. Invest in a good, professional head shot taken in executive style. Wear business attire, and be sure to smile. Have enough copies made in 5" x 7" or 8" x 10" so you can send them out as needed. You will use the photo in all your promotional material.

Element Six: The Seminar Workbook. Nothing communicates professionalism as well as a well-designed workbook.

Element Seven: The Client list. Your credibility will be enhanced by a list of organizations that have benefited from your seminar. For example, when you market your program to corporations, list all the other corporations at which you have presented it. (Make sure this list is approved by your compliance department.)

Element Eight: Articles or books. Include copies of any articles or books you have written. This is a powerful way to build credibility.

Element Nine: Press clippings. This includes anything written about you or articles in which you are cited as an expert or quoted.

Element Ten: A Video or audio demo tape. If you have a professionally recorded video or audio tape that demonstrates your presentation skills, include it.

Element Eleven: A Web site. If you have a Web site, promote it in your media kit.

How to Package Your Media Kit for Maximum Impact
In the past all of the above materials were produced in a hard-copy form. Today

everything in a media can be delivered digitally except for a book if you have written one.

You can post all of the elements of your media kit on your website. You might want to create some in hard-copy form for instances when it is requested.

If you are assembling a hard-copy media kit is worth your investment to put the components of your media kit together in such a way that it has perceived value. The best way to do this is to use a customized folder with pockets.

Folders customized with your logo and company name are a good investment that can last a lifetime, assuming the name of your company does not change. Use folders with a precut slot on the inside to hold your business card for contact information.

Here's a great company that specializes in customized business folders.

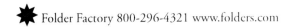 Folder Factory 800-296-4321 www.folders.com

CHAPTER 15.
IDENTIFYING YOUR MOST
LUCRATIVE IN-HOUSE
OPPORTUNITY

Consider each of the seven primary in-house opportunities, and then decide which ones best fit your products and services and your target market.

Professional and Trade Associations

There are approximately ten thousand trade and professional associations in the United States and more than ten thousand local, regional, and state associations. Almost every adult in America belongs to at least one association, if not several.

Associations need seminar leaders to provide educational programs for their members, and they are almost always open to suggestions. Here again, your target audience becomes your guide in choosing which associations to pursue. When you customize your materials to a specific target audience, you heighten your chances of success.

Figure out where your expertise lies, and approach the associations you feel could benefit most from your seminar. Some associations operate only on a national level, while others hold local meetings in particular regions, states, counties, or cities.

Talking to your existing clients offers the best way to choose which associations to market your presentation to. Ask clients what professional organizations they belong to. For example, if one of your ideal clients is a real estate professional, ask this person what local real estate associations would be appropriate for you to approach.

You can also look under associations in the Yellow Pages of your local telephone directory. You will find a list of many associations that are nearby. Go through them carefully to figure out which ones are good prospects for you. Some of them may not be professional associations, and some may not have meetings with speakers. Identify the ones whose members would be good prospects for your products and services.

Columbia Books listed below offer complete directories of professional and trade associations. They're loaded with background information. You can find them in the business section at most libraries.

Columbia Books, Inc.
www.columbiabooks.com
Columbia Books publishes two directories:
National Trade and Professional Associations of the US
State and Regional Associations of the United States

Adult and Continuing Education Programs
Practically every college and university in America offers a noncredit continuing education program. This same type of programs is offered by high schools, libraries, organizations like YMCA and YMHA, and even park and recreational facilities.

In addition, there are thousands of private adult education organizations that offer courses in everything from flower arranging to sushi making. These organizations offer great opportunities for you to present your financial seminar.

Start by identifying the organizations that offer adult and continuing educational programs in your area, and call or write for their catalogs. Evaluate each organization's current curriculum and identify a portion for your seminar.

> If you present your program at a college or university, ask if they will give you camera-ready copy or a JPEG of their institutional logo so that you can print it on your brochure. This will lend credibility to your seminar and increase registration.

Service and Fraternal Organizations

Many service clubs and fraternal organizations, such as Rotary, Kiwanis, Elks, and Lions Clubs, need speakers. They look for people who can deliver short presentations at luncheon, dinner, and evening meetings.

You must be able to deliver a lively talk that contains information relevant to that specific group. These organizations could be ideal for you if their members fit your target audience.

Church and Religious Groups

These organizations offer a variety of personal development programs. They have a sincere commitment to improve all aspects of their members' lives.

Your ideal starting point is with your own religious affiliation. Once you've done a good job for one group, collect endorsements, and you'll be able to book lots of these inhouse seminars. You can then expand to a whole circuit.

If your target group is based on shared values, church groups offer a natural market for you. You will enjoy working with these groups, and you will be able to communicate to them based on your shared values.

Corporate Programs

More corporations now rely on financial industry professionals to provide financial advice and support to their employees than ever before. As more employees take their financial future into their own hands, corporations and businesses will be relieved of responsibility to provide support.

Marketing your seminar to corporations requires a diligent approach. Here are some guidelines and tips. You'll need corporate approval to implement some of them.

1. Decision makers are difficult to find: persevere.
2. The human resource department is usually the best place to begin.
3. Third party endorsements and referrals are invaluable.
4. Workbooks and materials are critical for credibility.
5. Emphasize that there will be no selling of products or services during your seminar.
6. Focus your comments on the educational nature of your seminar.
7. On-site breakfast and lunch seminars are the easiest to schedule.

8. Ask for promotional help in the form of a company-wide memo or e-mail.
9. Put up flyers or posters on the company bulletin boards.
10. Write an article for the organization's newsletter.
11. Insert a flyer in the newsletter.
12. Distribute flyers in employee mail boxes.
13. Request promotional materials to be stuffed in pay envelopes.
14. Provide refreshments.
15. Adapt the presentation to issues specific to the organization.
16. Talk to someone in human resources for help in customizing your script.

Senior Centers and Senior Living Communities
Many of these are upscale groups whose members seek financial advice in a variety of areas. These groups are always looking for speakers. Many senior centers and communities have several different facilities operated by the same company. If you do a good job at one, they will endorse you, and you will be offered lots of opportunities.

Nonprofit Organizations
Many nonprofits conduct meetings in your area; their members might be perfect audiences for your products and services. For example, nonprofit parent and school groups might be interested in your seminar to help with financial planning for their children's future educational needs.

CHAPTER 16.
THE IN-HOUSE SEMINAR
SUCCESS PLAN

The marketing plan for in-house seminars does not have a clear time line as the plans for client-event seminars and public seminars do.

The organization's meeting schedule determines your schedule for marketing the in-house seminar. Even though you do not control the time line, the steps are clearly defined.

The Winning Marketing System: PEP

Using PEP, the Phone-Email-Phone system, makes it easy to market your seminar to organizations.

Phone. Make your initial contact with the organization by phone. Identify and contact the decision maker, qualify the organization, gain involvement, and set up a next step.

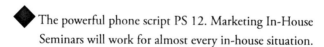 The powerful phone script PS 12. Marketing In-House
Seminars will work for almost every in-house situation.

Email. Email your media kit with the promotional materials described in Chapter 14.

Phone. Follow-up is the essential element to getting the booking. About a week to ten days after you email your material to the decision-maker, follow up with a phone call.

Many of the decision makers in noncorporate organizations are volunteers;

others do not consider your seminar a top priority. Often you perform a service for them by reminding them about the availability of your presentation.

◢◢ Whenever possible, meet with the decision maker in person. If you are marketing to a local group, you can even attend one of their meetings.

Always keep in mind when you market your seminar to organizations: They need you. They need speakers and presenters. So persevere.

◆ Use PS 13. In-House Follow-Up, found in Chapter 18, as an effective phone script after you have sent your materials to the decision maker.

Organize all your prospects for in-house seminars. Use your contact management program to keep track of materials sent and follow-up calls made to each in-house opportunity. Schedule your follow-up activities, and perform them religiously.

◢◢ Invite decision makers for in-house opportunities to one of your client event or public seminars or speaking engagements so they can see you live. Your performance makes a great marketing tool.

◢◢ Whenever you speak to a group, collect the names, addresses, and phone numbers of participants for your mailing list, so that you can invite them to future events. The easiest way to get this information is to have attendees fill out cards for a drawing to win a free book or other resource related to your presentation.

Getting Paid to Sell Your Services

Some organizations will offer you a fee to speak to their group. For example, most adult and continuing education organizations and many religious organizations offer some form of compensation for presentations.

If a nonprofit or service organization offers a fee, consider donating it to a charity connected to that organization. Doing so will give a huge boost to your relationship with the group.

 Use MD 14. Letter of Agreement for In-House Speaking Engagement, found in Chapter 19, when you are booked to present your seminar in-house. It is helpful to use this agreement even if no fee is involved.

PART FIVE: CREATING NEW BUSINESS OPPORTUNITIES

You will maximize your new business opportunities if you implement effective closing strategies and techniques.

CHAPTER 17.
HOW TO MASTER THE ART OF
CLOSING APPOINTMENTS

Learn the proven strategies presented here and you are bound to create new business opportunities.

Focusing on the Contact Points
Regardless of the type of seminar you market and present, focus on the points of contact between you and your prospects. These contact points will either attract prospects or push them away. Here are the critical contact points that make a difference in your closing ratios.

1. Your marketing material. Your invitations, brochures, and other materials should represent you in the most professional manner. They should speak to your target market.

2. Registration. Your telephones should be answered in a professional manner. The people answering should use a script and speak in a friendly, upbeat manner. Every registrant should be made to feel special and important.

    If you use a phone service to take reservations and make confirmation calls, call in yourself as a mystery shopper. Test your service more than once to make sure your registrants are consistently treated with high quality.

3. The confirmation letter. Your confirmation letter should convey professionalism and create the right image of you and your company.

4. The confirmation phone call. You can use this call to gather information, establish rapport, and qualify prospects. This point of contact should motivate them to show up at the event.

5. At the seminar, before it begins. Use this time to initiate relationships with the participants. Ask questions. Express interest in them and their issues.

6. During the seminar. Make your seminar interactive and conversational. Participation helps build relationships.

7. After the seminar. Plan to stay around after the seminar to answer questions and continue to build relationships with the participants.

Closing Strategies and Techniques That Work

You will get many more appointments if you employ effective strategies throughout the seminar selling process.

New business is the fruit of your marketing plan, but the appointment is the fruit of the seminar. The secret is to begin announcing the appointment early and in various ways. None of the closing techniques that follow can be considered a hard sell. Use them when you conduct public seminars.

The Pre-event Appointment Close for Public Seminars. Plant the seeds for the appointment by announcing it in your marketing material. The method for doing so is to include the following copy: All attendees will be offered a FREE one-hour consultation.

The response to your brochure, letter, flyer, or advertisement may decrease as a result of including this offer at the bottom of the piece. But most people who don't respond because of this statement would probably not be good prospects for an appointment anyway.

The Check-In-Table Close. It is easy to place a sign on or next to the check-in table that announces the availability of the free consultation. The sign should say: Participants will be offered a free office consultation at the end of this seminar.

The negative effect of this announcement is somewhat measurable. Very few people will refuse to enter the seminar because of this announcement. The sign prepares them for the inevitable. When you do finally ask for the commitment to set an appointment, both you and your participants are likely to feel more comfortable.

It is worth investing a few dollars at a local sign shop; have a sign made that can be placed right where attendees pick up materials and sign in.

The Before-We-Start Close. After your participants are seated and you have been introduced and have thanked the participants for attending the seminar, you can introduce the appointment by following this simple process:

Ask participants to take out the materials they received when they checked-in. Ask them to locate the "Participant Questionnaire" or "Seminar Evaluation" sheet. Then say, "Some of you might want to leave early. To avoid wasting time at the conclusion of the program, please fill in your name, address, and phone number now. Please note the section for scheduling an appointment in my office. I'll tell you more about that at the end of the program."

The Complimentary Consultation Document. When you have completed the body of your seminar, it is time to ask participants to make an appointment. The written request for an appointment is on your questionnaire or evaluation form. Although different in style, each of the three closing documents described below can be customized in any way that feels most comfortable for you. Feel free to mix and match parts from each one. You will find the three documents in Chapter 19.

◆ MD 15. Participant Questionnaire – Closing Document
has an outstanding feature: the participant can request a
specific date and time.

◆ MD 16. Free 45-Minute Review – Closing Document
can be completed very quickly. It must be customized for
your specific products and services.

◆ MD 17. Short Evaluation – Appointment Document
can also be completed quickly, but it asks for comments
and referrals.

You can set appointments using one of the complimentary consultation documents, or you can ask participants to go to the back of the room and schedule their appointment with a staff member. You will need at least one assistant to handle the appointment sheets. Once an appointment has been set, give the prospect an appointment confirmation sheet.

◆ MD 18. Appointment Confirmation Form, in Chapter 19, is a sample you can copy.

⚡ While participants fill out the questionnaire or go to the back of the room to sign up for an appointment, you can stage a question-and-answer period.

The Million-Dollar Close. As mentioned earlier, the most significant drawback to delivering in-house seminars is the lack of freedom to ask for business. But the milliondollar closing technique, when used at in-house seminars, will bring you qualified leads every time.

Sponsoring organizations invite you to educate their members, not to sell your products or services. Many organizations specify that although they really appreciate your providing education, they want you to refrain from any direct selling.

The trick is to provide a response mechanism that is not perceived as a sales pitch and that will let you leave every in-house seminar with qualified leads, some of whom will become clients.

Never ever deliver an in-house seminar without using the million-dollar closing technique. Here's the powerful script for this special close:

> Before I close, I'd like to thank you for giving me the opportunity to speak to you today. I know I haven't covered everything about taking control of your financial future. If there is anybody here who would like more information about how to design a financial plan based on what's important to you and how we can help you put that plan together, please take out a business card now. Write the letters "PSS" on the front. That stands for Personal Seminar Service. And when I'm done in a few minutes, please give your card to me. I promise I'll personally get back to you within the next day or two.

Some groups, such as residents of senior communities or retirees, might not have business cards. In these instances, provide each participant with two of your business cards before you begin. Then, during the million-dollar close, ask all those who want more information to write their name and telephone number on one of your cards and give it back to you.

The Follow-Up Call. Everyone who attended your seminar must be called afterwards. The follow-up call helps you book more appointments. It also helps you to determine how qualified a participant is or when to check back.

◆ PS 14. Seminar Follow-up, a phone script found in Chapter 18, is effective for following up with participants.

You also need to call all of the no-shows. You may be able to qualify some of them and set some appointments.

◆ The phone script PS 15. Follow-up for No-show, found in Chapter 18, can help you to maximize your results.

Confirm Consultations. All of the participants who signed up for a complimentary consultation need to be confirmed by telephone and by mail. This will reduce the noshow rate for appointments.

◆ PS 16. Appointment Confirmation Call, in Chapter 18, lets you confirm the details of the appointment, reflect your professionalism, and strengthen your relationship with the prospect.

◆ MD 19. Appointment Confirmation Letter, in Chapter 19, provides all the particulars of the appointment.

PART SIX: MARKETING RESOURCES

This part contains all the tools – phone scripts and marketing document templates – you need for marketing via telephone and mail.

CHAPTER 18.
PHONE SCRIPTS

_____(name), I'm calling to invite you and your wife and a guest or two to a very special seminar on _____(date). This program will show you how to create a financial plan based on what's important to you. You learn how to feel confident that you are making wise decisions about your money. As you probably know, a sound financial plan is critical to security for you and your family.

The seminar called Taking Control of Your Financial Future will provide you with fundamentals of the financial planning process. It is free, and it will run about ninety minutes. We'll also be serving some delicious refreshments.

We would be honored to have you as our guest at _____ (location) on _____(date) at _____(time).

(Choose and use here a Referral Generation Script, PS 2, PS 3, or PS 4.)

I'm excited about seeing you at _____(location, date, time). I'll mail you a confirmation letter with all the details and call you back in a few days to get the names of your friends who will be attending the event.

What is a convenient time to get back to you?

And once again, I want to thank you for taking the time to call your friends to invite them to our client seminar.

PS 2. PHONE SCRIPT FOR REFERRAL GENERATION

_____(name), I'm not sure if you know this, but you are one of my favorite clients. In fact, I wish all my clients were like you. Who do you know who is also a _____(target market) like you and might enjoy attending a seminar like this?

(If they come up with a few names, continue.)

(If the client has difficulty identifying referrals, see PS 6. Phone Script for Handling Referral Objections.)

_____(name), I need your help. I'd like you to call_____
_____(names of referrals) and invite them and their spouses to our seminar event. I'll call you back in a few days to find out who will be attending.

PS 3. PHONE SCRIPT FOR REFERRAL GENERATION (ALTERNATE 1)

_____(name), as you probably know, my business has been built on word-of-mouth advertising. This seminar is a perfect opportunity for me to meet friends and associates of yours in a pleasant, relaxed environment.

They will learn about our approach to financial management, our expertise, and our philosophy. And then they can decide if they would like to learn more about our services. Who do you know who might enjoy attending this seminar?

(After they come up with a few names, continue.)

(If the client has difficulty identifying referrals, see PS 6. Phone Script for Handling Referral Objections.)

_____(name), I need your help. I'd like you to call _____(names of referrals) and invite them and their spouses to our seminar event. I'll call you back in a few days to find out who will be attending.

PS 4. PHONE SCRIPT FOR REFERRAL GENERATION (ALTERNATE 2)

_____(name), our goal is to grow our business, and the best way we've found to do this is with referrals. This seminar is the easiest way for us to meet friends of yours without putting them under any pressure. Who do you know who would enjoy attending this very special seminar event?

(After they come up with a few names, continue.)

(If the client has difficulty identifying referrals, see PS 6. Phone Script for Handling Referral Objections.)

_____(name), I need your help. I'd like you to call _____ (names of referrals) and invite them and their spouses to our seminar event. I'll call you back in a few days to find out who will be attending.

_____(name), I'm calling to find out who you'll be bringing as a guest to our upcoming seminar.

(If the client gives you names, continue with this script.)

(If the client has difficulty identifying referrals, see PS 6. Phone Script for Handling Referral Objections.)

Great! I'd like to get their contact information so we can confirm all the details of the event.

What's their name, address, and phone number?

Would it be OK for someone from our office to phone them to confirm their attendance?

(If yes , see PS 7. Phone Script for Confirming Referral.)

(If no, see MD 2. Letter for Confirming Referral.)

I can understand how it's sometimes hard to think of specific names right off the top of your head.

Maybe if we brainstorm for a minute, we can think of a few people who will enjoy this great seminar experience.

As you know, we specialize in helping _____(target market).

(Continue by focusing on specific groups who might fit your target market. Below are seven examples.)

Who do you know who

     is a small business owner like you?

     is also a member of the Chamber of Commerce like you?

     is also a member of your church?

     loves to play golf the way you do?

     is also a member of the Rotary Club?

     is also retired like you?

     is also a sales executive planning for retirement?

Hi, _____(referral's name).

My name is _____(your name) with _____(your firm). We have a mutual friend, _____(client's name). I was pleased to find out that you and your spouse will be attending our upcoming workshop, Taking Control of Your Financial Future.

I am calling to confirm the details for the event. It will be on _____ (day, date, time) at _____(location).

We have enjoyed serving and working with _____(client's name) and look forward to meeting you.

I'm confident you will find this seminar to be an informative and enlightening experience.

(Engage in some conversation to build rapport and strengthen the relationship.)

We will be sending you a letter confirming the details. I'm looking forward to seeing you on _____(day, date) at _____(time).

PS 8. PHONE SCRIPT FOR TAKING A RESERVATION

_____(company name), _____(name) speaking. How may I help you?

I'd like to register for your upcoming seminar.

Great! Which date are you looking at?

The one on Thursday the 22nd.

Wonderful. Can I get your name and information please?

(Get name, address, e-mail, etc.)

And how many are in your party?

Just two, my wife and I.

_____(participant's name), I'm sure you and your wife are going to thoroughly enjoy this informative and enlightening seminar.

_____(your name) is always looking to customize his remarks. Can I ask you a few questions to help us do that?

1. Have you attended any other financial seminars?

2. (If yes) What didn't you like about it?

3. What concerns you most about your financial plan?

4. Do you currently handle your own financial affairs, or do you use professionals?

5. Is there anything in particular you would like to have covered?

Thank you so much for helping us with this feedback, _____(name).

Who else do you know who might be interested in attending this program?

Perhaps my daughter and son-in-law.

I'd be happy to reserve two more spots for you. When should I get back to you to confirm those tickets?

(Take information and follow up accordingly.)

Hello, _____ (participant). I'm just calling to confirm the attendance of you and your wife at our upcoming financial seminar, Taking control of Your Financial Future, on _____(day/date) at _____(location) beginning at _____(time).

Did you receive the confirmation letter we sent you? Are you still planning to attend?

_____(participant's name), I'm sure you and your wife are going to thoroughly enjoy this informative and enlightening seminar. _____ (your name) is always looking to customize his remarks. Can I ask you a few questions to help us do that?

1. Have you attended any other financial seminars?
2. (If yes) What didn't you like about it?
3. What concerns you most about your financial plan?
4. Do you currently handle your own financial affairs, or do you use professionals?
5. Is there anything in particular you would like to have covered? Thank you so much for helping us with this feedback, _____(name).

Who else do you know who might be interested in attending this program? We still have a few seats available at the seminar.

Perhaps my daughter and son-in-law

I'd be happy to reserve two more spots for you. When should I get back to you to confirm those tickets?

(Take information.)

I am really looking forward to seeing you both. I'm sure you will appreciate the seminar, enjoy the _____(food/refreshments), and have a great time. I'll check back with you next week to confirm those additional reservations.

Hello, _____(registrant's name), this is _____(name) calling from _____(company). I'm calling to confirm your attendance at the Taking Control of Your Financial Futurse seminar that will be held tomorrow _____(day, date).

We have you registered as a party of _____(number of people). Check-in begins at _____(time) and the program will begin promptly at _____(time).

(If they cancel, say) I'm sorry you can't attend. Would you like to make an appointment to meet personally with _____(your name)?

(If they say yes, continue.)

May I help you with directions?

Do you have any questions I can answer?

Great! See you tomorrow at _____(time).

Hello. May I please speak with _____(potential participant's name).
That's me.

(Potential participant's name)_____, my name is _____
(your name) and I'm with _____(your company). Are you familiar with
our firm?

I don't think so.

Well, I'm calling to invite you to a very special financial seminar that will
be given right near you at _____(seminar site). This seminar is designed to
help you achieve long-term financial security. Is this something you might enjoy
learning more about?

Sounds interesting.

Well, we know making sound financial decisions has never been easy, and
with the ever-changing financial world, it is even more difficult.

At our seminar, you will learn how to make smart decisions about your
money. You will learn how to design a financial plan based on what's important
to you. As you probably know, a sound financial plan is critical to security for
you and your family.

This seminar, Taking Control of Your Financial Future, is free, and we will
be serving a complimentary _____(food or refreshment). Does this
sound like something that might be worthwhile for you?

It sounds pretty good. When did you say it is?

It's going to be on _____(date) at _____(time) at _____(location). Is
that a convenient date for you?

(If no, give an alternate date, and then continue.)

(If yes, continue.)

We'll mail out an invitation package today. Let me make sure I have your
information correct. (Check spelling of name and address.)

You'll be receiving a call in a few days to confirm your attendance.

That's sounds fine.

Thank you, and we look forward to seeing you on _____(date).

Hi, my name is _____(your name). I'm with _____(your company). I'd like to speak to the person in charge of providing _____(your members, your group, your employees, etc.) with personal financial planning information.

(Because you may be connected to the incorrect person the first time, introduce yourself again, and confirm that you are speaking to the right person.)

Are you the person in charge of providing _____(your members, your group, your employees, etc.) with personal financial planning information?

(You will probably have to provide more information about what you do and your presentation. Prepare a short description of your seminar and describe a benefit. For example, you might say:

I'd like the opportunity to provide information that will help members of your organization take control of their financial future. We will provide an educational program that will help them achieve that goal.

After you are sure that you are speaking to a qualified decision maker, qualify the current needs of the organization for seminars or presentations.)

Do you currently provide educational programs or use speakers at your meetings?

(If no, thank them for their time, and move on.)

(If yes, continue.)

What do I have to do to be considered to present my program at your _____(church, association, corporation)?

(At this point, the decision maker will describe the procedures and possible opportunities for you to present your seminar or presentation. For example, he or she might say something like this:

We do offer lunchtime seminars at our company. Sometimes we use speakers at our monthly meeting. My job is to bring possible programs to our program committee that meets every month. Is there anything you can send us?)

(Confirm your next step.)

I am going to mail you a media kit that will include some background material on my organization, my seminar program, Taking Control of Your Financial Future, and me. I must emphasize that I will not do any hard selling of our financial products and services, but I would like to make my services available to those who would like more help.

Hi, _____ (prospect's name), this is _____(your name) with _____(your company). I am just calling to find out whether you've received the material I mailed to you and to see whether you've had a chance to review it.

(If the answer is no, continue with)

When would be the best time to get back to you?

(If the answer is yes, continue with)

Does this program look like something that could serve _____(the members of your organization, employees of your company, etc.)?

(If the answer is yes, continue with)

What's the next best step?

(The decision maker will lay out the procedures. It might have to go to a committee or be reviewed by someone else at a higher level. After you are clear on the next step, say)

So, when should I check in with you again?

(Do not accept a vague time; instead, pinpoint a specific date that will be appropriate for you to call back.)

(If the person says, "I'll get back to you," ask when you should expect a call. Then say)

Great! If I don't hear from you by _____(first date), I will call you back on _____(second date).

Hi, _____ (name). I'm calling from _____(your firm) to thank you for attending our seminar. We're glad you could make it. Did you enjoy it?

Yes, thanks.

Great!

I just wanted to give you a courtesy call since we haven't heard from you. I would love to get together with you to show you what we do here. Would you like to take advantage of our free consultation to see if there is any way we can help you design a financial plan based on what's important to you?

Hi, _____(name). I'm calling from _____(your firm). You were signed up for our seminar, and we were disappointed that you couldn't make it. What was it that attracted you to sign up for the seminar?

(Listen for the problem, need, or concern.)

You know, that was one of the topics we covered in the seminar. (Offer some insights or possible solutions.)

It's hard to give you in-depth answers to your problems without knowing more about your situation. We did offer complimentary consultations at the seminar.

Why don't we set a time for you to come in and see if we can help. There is no obligation, and we can find out if our services fit your needs.

(Wait for a response.) (

If yes, set an appointment.)

(If no, say)

Why don't you plan to attend our next seminar on _____(date). Would you like us to send you an invitation?

Hi, _____(participant's name), this is _____(your name) with
_____(your firm). You attended our seminar on _____
(date) at _____(location). How did you like the seminar?

I really enjoyed it.

Great!

You requested a call to make an appointment for a complimentary consultation. I'm calling to arrange a time. (Set the appointment.)

(or)

You made an appointment for a complimentary consultation. We have you down for _____(day and time). Is that still convenient for you?

Is there anyone else you would like to bring with you?

(Put the names of the additional people in the contact management system.)

As you know, this is a free consultation, and you will be under no obligation whatsoever. We do ask you to bring with you the information we need to get a better understanding of how we can serve you and if we are a good fit.

(Review the documents you need the person to bring in.)

We have you down for _____(day) at _____(time). We look forward to seeing you.

CHAPTER 19.
MARKETING DOCUMENTS

MD 1. Client Invitation Letter

MD 2. Referral Confirmation Letter

MD 3. Referral Invitation Letter

MD 4. Confirmation Letter for Clients and Referrals

MD 5. Public Seminar Invitation Copy

MD 6. Post-Paid Reply Postcard

MD 7. Public Seminar Tickets

MD 8. Seminar Confirmation Letter

MD 9. Newspaper Advertisement or Insert – Black-and-White Version

MD 10. Newspaper Advertisement or Insert – Full Color Version

MD 11. Sample Calendar Announcement

MD 12. Media Kit Cover Letter

MD 13. In-House Program Description

MD 14. Letter of Agreement for In-House Speaking Engagement

MD 15. Participant Questionnaire – Closing Document

MD 16. Free 45-Minute Review – Closing Document

MD 17. Short Evaluation – Appointment Document

MD 18. Appointment Confirmation Form

MD 19. Appointment Confirmation Letter

MD 20. Call Tracking Sheet

(your letterhead)

_____(date)

Dear _____(client name):

I'd like to invite you to a special event on financial planning. This is a program for our preferred clients and their guests.

As you know, making financial decisions has never been more confusing or difficult. Our seminar will provide you with answers to the following questions:

- How do I know if I am making smart decisions about my money?
- Are my financial decisions based on what's really important to me?
- Am I clear about my financial goals?
- Are my financial affairs organized properly?

Attend this free, powerful, ninety-minute special seminar and you will discover a successful approach for making informed and intelligent decisions about managing your money.

The Taking Control of Your Financial Future seminar will be held on _____(day),_____(date), from _____(time) to _____(time) at _____(location).

Please call me today at _____ (phone number) to reserve your place at this important event.

Sincerely,

_____(your signature)

_____(your typed name)

(your letterhead)

_____(date)

Dear _____(referral's name):

We are so pleased that you have accepted _____(your client's name) invitation and will be attending our informative seminar, Taking Control of Your Financial Future , on _____(day), _____(date), from _____ (time) to _____(time) at _____(location).

The seminar will provide you with answers to the following questions:

- How do I know if I am making smart decisions about my money?
- Are my financial decisions based on what's really important to me?
- Am I clear about my financial goals?
- Are my financial affairs organized properly?

There is no charge for this powerful hour-and-a-half seminar. You will discover a successful approach for making informed and intelligent decisions about managing your money.

We value our relationship with _____(client's name), and we look forward to meeting you and sharing this time together.

Sincerely,

_____(your signature)

_____(your typed name)

PS Please call _____(phone number) if you would like to add someone to the guest list.

(your letterhead)

_____(date)

Dear _____(referral's name):

_____(client's name) suggested that I invite you to a special upcoming seminar, Taking Control of Your Financial Future. _____(client's name) is one our preferred clients and feels you might find great value in what you will learn at this program. It is free for our preferred clients and their guests.

We understand that making financial decisions has never been more confusing or difficult. This seminar will provide you with the answers to the following questions:

- How do I know if I am making smart decisions about my money?
- Are my financial decisions based on what's really important to me?
- Am I clear about my financial goals?
- Are my financial affairs organized properly?

In this powerful, free, 90-minute seminar, discover a successful approach for making informed, intelligent decisions about managing your money.

We value our relationship with _____(client's name), and we look forward to meeting you and sharing this time together.

Please call me today at _____ (phone number) to confirm your place at this important event.

Sincerely,

_____(your signature)

_____(your typed name)

(your letterhead)

Reservation Confirmation

_____(date)

_____(participant's name)

_____(participant's address)

Dear _____(participant's name):

We are so pleased that you have accepted our invitation and will be attending our informative seminar, Taking Control of Your Financial Future, on _____(day, date) from _____(time) to _____(time) at _____(location).

All materials, including workbooks, will be provided for the seminar. We will start promptly at _____(time).

We are confident that this program will exceed your expectations, and we look forward to seeing you.

Sincerely,

_____(your signature)

_____(your typed name)

Learn the Secrets of Managing Your Money Successfully

Making sound financial decisions has never been easy. In the ever-changing financial world, it is even more difficult. With so many investment products, personal financial concerns, and changing tax laws, it is no wonder that most people are confused about their money.

We would like to invite you to a FREE seminar designed to help you achieve longterm financial security. This seminar, Taking Control of Your Financial Future, will provide you with answers to the following questions:

- How do I know if I am making smart decisions about my money?
- Are my financial decisions based on what's really important to me?
- Am I clear about my financial goals?
- Are my financial affairs organized properly?

There is no charge for this learning experience. You owe it to yourself and your family to attend this program. Discover a successful approach to managing your money.

Your presenter is _____(your name). _____(bio and photo).

Four complimentary tickets are enclosed. Please call us today at _____ (toll free phone number), open 24/7, or complete and mail the enclosed reply card to reserve your place at this important event. We promise that this is an educational seminar and that you will be under no obligation of any kind.

Taking Control of Your Financial Future

_____(day)

_____(date)

_____(time) to _____(time)

_____(location)

Seating is limited. Reservations are required. You must RSVP by _____ (date).

Call toll free _____(phone number) or mail the enclosed reply card today!

[ ] Yes. Please reserve a seat for me at your seminar, Taking Control of Your Financial Future, to be held on _____(day, date) at _____ (time). There will be _____people attending, including me.

[ ] I will not be able to attend this seminar, but I am interested in a complimentary consultation.

Name _____

Address _____

City _____ State _____ Zip _____

Day Phone _____ Evening Phone _____

(Front)

Admission Ticket

Taking Control of Your Financial Future

Complimentary Admission

This ticket is valid for two (2) complimentary admissions.

See reverse side for workshop information.

(Back)

_____(your company) presents the seminar

Taking Control of Your Financial Future

Your Presenter: _____

Day: _____

Date: _____

Time: _____

Location: _____

For more information, please call _____(toll free phone number).

Reservation Confirmation

_____(date)

Dear _____(participant name):

We look forward to your participation in our upcoming seminar, Taking Control of Your Financial Future.

Date: _____

Check in: _____(time)

Seminar: from _____(start time) to _____(finish time)

Location: _____

All program materials, including the workbook, will be provided at the seminar. Please allow enough time to check in and receive your materials.

We appreciate your attendance at this seminar, and we are confident that this will be an extremely worthwhile investment of your time.

We look forward to seeing you very soon.

Sincerely,

_____(your signature)

_____(your typed name)

Making sound financial decisions has never been easy. In the ever-changing financial world, it is even more difficult. With so many investment products, personal financial concerns, and changing tax laws, it is no wonder that most people are confused about their money.

You are invited to a FREE seminar designed to help you achieve long-term financial security. This seminar, Taking Control of Your Financial Future, will provide you with answers to these questions:

- How do I know if I am making smart decisions about my money?
- Are my financial decisions based on what's really important to me?
- Am I clear about my financial goals?
- Are my financial affairs organized properly?

There is no charge for this learning experience. You owe it to yourself and your family to attend this program. Discover a successful approach to managing your money.

Please join us for this free seminar: Taking Control of Your Financial Future. Learn how to make informed and intelligent decisions about managing your money. This is an educational seminar, with no obligation of any kind. We will not discuss any product.

(bio and photo)
(day, date)
(time to time)
(location)
(phone number)
(Your firm's name, logo, and address)
Seats are FREE. Reservations are required. Call today!!

Red Dragon Financial Services
2516 Highland Ave.
Palos Verdes, CA 90269

Contact: Alan Cain (800) 794-8072

For Immediate Release

Discover a successful approach to making informed and intelligent decisions about managing your money. Find out how to organize your financial affairs successfully. This FREE seminar, Taking Control of Your Financial Future, will be held at Barnaby's Hotel in Palos Verdes on Wednesday, May 7. Your presenter will be Nancy Diesmone, president of Red Dragon Financial Services.

For more information or to register, call Alan Cain at (800) 794-8072.

(your letterhead)

_____(date)

_____(decision maker)

_____(decision maker's address)

Dear _____(decision maker):

Thank you for your interest in our presentation, Taking Control of Your Financial Future. As I mentioned to you on the phone, this program will be customized to your needs.

The materials you asked for are enclosed.

I look forward to speaking with you again after you've had a chance to review our materials – and I welcome the possibility of serving you and your group.

Sincerely,

_____(your signature)

_____(your typed name)

Taking Control of Your Financial Future

Making sound financial decisions has never been easy. In the ever-changing financial world, it is even more difficult. With so many investment products, personal financial concerns, and changing tax laws, it is no wonder that most people are confused about their money.

This presentation is designed to help you achieve long-term financial security. It will provide you with answers to the following questions:

- How do I know if I am making smart decisions about my money?
- Are my financial decisions based on what's really important to me?
- Am I clear about my financial goals?
- Are my financial affairs organized properly?

MD 14. LETTER OF AGREEMENT FOR IN-HOUSE SPEAKING ENGAGEMENT

(your letterhead)

LETTER of AGREEMENT
between

_____(your company) and _____(organization)

Dear _____(contact name):

Subject: _____(your presentation title)

_____(your name) will speak to your group on _____ (date). The location will be _____(hotel or meeting facility) in _____(City), _____(State). The presentation, Taking Control of Your Financial Future, will be _____(hours, minutes) in length. It will begin at _____(time) and end at _____(time).

The fee for this presentation will be _____(dollar amount) plus expenses, which include roundtrip airfare from _____(airport) in _____(city, state); hotel; meals; and ground transportation.

No tape recorder, audio or video, may be used during the presentation without prior written permission of _____(your company).

Upon receipt of a ten percent deposit of _____(dollar amount) and this signed letter, the proposed date will be reserved for you.

The balance of _____(dollar amount) will be given to _____ (your company) prior to the presentation. All expenses will be billed.

_____(your company) _____(organization)

_____, President _____, President

Date_____ Date_____

Participant Questionnaire Please print.

Name _____ Spouse _____

Address _____

City, State, Zip _____

Home Phone _____ Work Phone _____

What part of today's program did you find most valuable?

_____

_____

Based on today's program, what is your biggest financial concern?

_____

_____

☐   Yes, I would like to schedule a complimentary consultation.

Select a day: Circle a time:

_____ Monday 10:30 a.m. 12:30 p.m. 2:30 p.m.

_____ Tuesday 10:30 a.m. 12:30 p.m. 2:30 p.m.

_____ Wednesday 10:30 a.m. 12:30 p.m. 2:30 p.m.

_____ Thursday 10:30 a.m. 12:30 p.m. 2:30 p.m.

_____ Friday 10:30 a.m. 12:30 p.m. 2:30 p.m.

☐   I would like to schedule this seminar for my club, church, or organization.

Name of organization: _____

☐   I have friends, relatives, or associates who would benefit from this seminar.

Name _____ Phone _____

Name _____ Phone _____

FREE 45-Minute Personal, Confidential Review

I want more information on:

[ ] Increasing my retirement income

[ ] Maximizing my investments

[ ] Tax planning

[ ] Reducing estate tax

[ ] Designing a financial plan

[ ] Living trusts

[ ] Increasing my after-tax interest income

[ ] College funding

[ ] Asset allocation

[ ] Long-term health care

[ ] IRA rollover/retirement distribution

[ ] Annuities

[ ] Charitable giving

[ ] Advanced investment principles

I would prefer my free one-hour confidential review to be set up:

Place: [ ] in my home Time: [ ] Mornings

[ ] in my office [ ] Afternoon

Name _____

Daytime Telephone (_____) _____

Evening Telephone (_____) _____

Seminar Evaluation

[ ] Yes, I am interested in scheduling the complimentary consultation.

[ ] No, I am not interested in scheduling the complimentary consultation.

Name _____

Address _____

City _____State _____ Zip _____

Home Phone _____Work Phone _____

Please call me to schedule an appointment at

Daytime Phone_____ Evening Phone_____

What did you find most valuable in this seminar? _____

_____

_____

What was the least useful? _____

_____

_____

Please list anyone you know who might benefit from this seminar.

Name: _____ Phone: _____

Name: _____ Phone: _____

Name: _____ Phone: _____

(your letterhead)

This is to confirm your appointment at our office.
We look forward to seeing you on
_____(day), _____(date), at _____(time).
Please bring the following documents with you:
[ ] Tax returns from the past two years
[ ] Most recent bank statements
[ ] Most recent brokerage statements
[ ] Most recent retirement account statements
[ ] Copies of any insurance or annuity policies
[ ] Copies of wills and trusts

Our address is: _____(your address)

Directions to our office: _____(directions)

(your letterhead)

_____(date)
_____(prospect's name)
_____(prospect's address)

Dear _____(prospect's name):

Thank you for attending our recent seminar.

This letter confirms our upcoming appointment on _____(day) at _____(time) at my office at _____(address).

As we discussed on the telephone, this is a free consultation with absolutely no obligation on your part. The purpose of this meeting is to answer any questions you might have and to see if we can help you with your financial needs.

To make this meeting worthwhile, please bring the documents we requested. These documents, listed below, will give us an accurate view of your current status.

[ ] Tax returns from the past two years

[ ] Most recent bank statements

[ ] Most recent brokerage statements

[ ] Most recent retirement account statements

[ ] Copies of any insurance or annuity policies

[ ] Copies of wills and trusts

Please call if you have any questions. I look forward to meeting you.

Sincerely,

_____(your signature)
_____(your typed name)

MD 20. CALL TRACKING SHEET

Caller: _____

Date: _____

Hours: _____ to _____

Calls	Contacts	Invitations Sent

CPSIA information can be obtained at www.ICGtesting.com
Printed in the USA
BVOW07s1504161013

333899BV00001B/1/P